IMPAIRED, BUT EMPOWERED

IMPAIRED, BUT EMPOWERED

A MEMOIR OF FAITH, FORTITUDE AND FORTUNE

Walter Ashby

Published by Up-Words Press
www.walterashby.com

ISBN 978–0-9983987–0-9

Cover Design: Summo Design
Editor: Cynthia Zigmund
Editorial Services: Second City Publishing, LLC

This book is dedicated to Gail for her years of love, support, and advocacy.
Love,
Walter, Beth Ann, and Becky

TABLE OF CONTENTS

FOREWORD

"The chief handicap of the blind is not blindness, but the attitude of seeing people towards them."

—Helen Keller

To be legally blind or visually impaired in this society is, in a sense, to be born between worlds. Many individuals who are legally blind feel they do not fit into either the "sighted" camp or the "blind" camp.

Most have enough vision to take part in the same activities as sighted persons, yet there are restrictions. Many cannot drive and almost all struggle with accessing the same print materials to which the average sighted person has access. Even in this technological age where such problems are diminishing, transportation and print access remain problems for most legally blind people.

And, because they are not totally blind, many persons who are legally blind do not learn Braille or use white canes.

The tendency for many individuals who are legally blind is to "pass as sighted." After all, the majority of the world's citizens are sighted. Sighted people make the rules, establish the norms, and set the standards. The sighted majority is the in-crowd and life is easier when you belong to the in-crowd.

Individuals who are legally blind know that being different is difficult. It means being singled out for special treatment and/or prejudicial acts. It may mean being subjected to pity, ridicule, or maltreatment. To avoid this, the easiest road for some is to work at being sighted.

However, for the legally blind person, denying vision loss and attempting to "pass as sighted" can be dangerous. One of my friends who was rapidly losing vision refused to use a white cane. He believed it made him look inferior and incapable. He changed his mind only after he had walked off a thirty-foot pier and almost drowned. Another friend continued to drive until she side-swiped a parked car.

Most individuals eventually come to the realization that blindness is a natural human condition. It presents challenges because the world is designed *by* sighted people *for* sighted people and includes some obstacles and barriers for someone who is blind. But all these obstacles can be mastered with the right application of training, tools, hard work, good problem-solving strategies, and a modicum of common sense.

Perhaps the grandest challenge for someone who is blind is dealing with inaccurate attitudes and beliefs held by both sighted and blind people in our society. As human beings in this society, we harbor many inaccurate beliefs and attitudes about blindness and blind persons, some of which can be formidable barriers to success for someone who is blind.

Where do these faulty beliefs and attitudes originate? Most of us get our ideas about blindness and blind persons from sources like the media, churches, and incidental meetings or sightings of blind people in the community. While some of these sources provide accurate information, most do not, or present only a portion of the picture, leaving us with inaccurate or incomplete information in our brain file labeled "Blindness." As a result, people who are blind frequently encounter attitudes and emotions in the community that reflect a skewed perspective. Here are some common reactions:

1. Fear: Some people are so frightened of going blind themselves they avoid blind persons altogether. Others feel awkward because they fear they will do the wrong thing and harm someone who is blind or do something to embarrass themselves.

2. Pity and Sympathy: Due to some religious teachings and the inaccurate portrayal of blind persons in the media, these reactions persist. My friend Sue shared this story of a time when she was standing outside a store waiting for friends: "As I was standing there, some well-intentioned human put their hand on my shoulder and said: 'There, but for the grace of God, go I.'" Persons who feel pity and sympathy for someone consider the object of their feelings to be inferior in some way.

3. Awe: Many persons who are blind report they occasionally meet someone who reacts in amazement at their simplest actions, e.g., "Wow!

You can tie your own shoelaces!" No doubt, that same person would not be astonished observing a sighted person completing the same task. Those who react in awe equate blindness with helplessness and have low expectations for someone who is blind. These individuals may be roadblocks to opportunity for a person who is blind because they believe a person with a disability will not be able to accomplish anything significant.

4. Anger: Some react in anger. These feelings often come from a place of low self-esteem. Individuals who do not feel good about themselves do not want anyone else to feel good either; so they engage in what I call "leveling." They seek to bring others "down to their level" or keep them "in their place." Individuals having anger may act as gate-keepers, blocking the way to activities, clubs, equal participation, or promotions and advancement. At the extremes, the angry person may engage in aggressive attacks like name-calling, bullying, and/or acts of violence. Some may employ a passive-aggressive approach and attempt to convince others that a person's disability is not as serious as reported. This strategy is designed to isolate or discredit a disabled person.

5. Acceptance: People who are blind also encounter those who accept them as equals. Accepting professionals listen well and provide needed or requested information, feedback, and guidance to individuals who are blind. The accepting person seeks to empower. Employees who are accepting treat their disabled colleagues as equal partners and expect the same participation from them as they would from any business associate.

The incidence of blindness in the population is slight enough that the average sighted person might never encounter someone who is blind, at least not on a personal basis where they could interact and correct their misconceptions about blindness. As a result, when they meet someone who is blind or welcome someone who is blind into their families most do not know how to react.

The best course for us all is simply to correct our misconceptions about blindness by adding more accurate information to our brain files. The most efficient and effective method for doing so is talking with successful individuals who are blind and have overcome many of the obstacles, misconceptions, prejudices, and attitudes described above.

I believe it is essential for children who are blind as well as their family members to get to know successful blind adults. It is equally essential for blindness professionals to become acquainted with successful persons in the community who are blind. This is the only real way to correct our misconceptions and change our perceptions about blindness and blind persons. We learn about blindness one person and one story at a time.

I am honored beyond words that Walter asked me to write this foreword. Walter is the reason I have invested more than forty years doing rehabilitation and training, most of it in the blindness field. He not only inspired me to investigate jobs in the field but he wrote a letter of commendation that helped me secure my first position in the field.

At Tarleton State University, where Walter and I first became friends and were roommates, I saw firsthand the struggles Walter, as a visually impaired student, faced on a daily basis:

1. Not having access to print materials.
2. Not having access to the same transportation options as other students.
3. Being underestimated by instructors and students who did not understand blindness or Walter's abilities.
4. Enduring blatant prejudice from faculty and students.
5. Being accused by some of faking his disability.
6. Being labeled "stuck up" because he did not always recognize people he passed on campus.

I also saw his outstanding abilities: intelligence, memory, organization, positive attitude, goal-setting, drive, the ability to control, manage and maximize his environment and any given situation, problem-solving difficult situations, and assertiveness.

In my years of service in the blindness field, I have observed many others struggling with similar issues. There is a lot of ignorance in the world about blindness and what it means to be blind. Blindness simply means a person cannot see or cannot see as well as the average human being. It doesn't change anything else about the individual.

Impaired, But Empowered is your chance to alter some of your own inaccurate ideas about what it means to be blind. Journey along with Walter as he shares his life story: experience with him the challenges and the joys of a successful person who is legally blind in a world designed by sighted people for sighted people. Along the way, you will learn new strategies you can use in your own lives whether you are disabled yourself or know someone who is—and regardless of the type of disability. And, I suspect, you will cheer for Walt as he negotiates the obstacles, whether imposed by society or by himself, to become extremely successful, in business, in the community, and most importantly, with his family. Enjoy and learn.

—Billy T. Brookshire
Chair, Governing Board, Hall of Fame for
Leaders and Legends of the Blindness Field

CHAPTER 1

JANIE

I was named Walter after my father, James Walter, whom we kids called Daddy. Turns out, this was a very fitting choice, as I was closer to him than any other family member. We seemed to think alike and he was, no doubt, the source of my intellect. Growing up in Mineral Wells, Texas, my childhood started out much like that of any other baby boomer. My mother (whom we called Mama), father, brother Jimmy, sister Janie, and I lived in a modest two-bedroom, one-bath white frame house on the outskirts of town. In most respects, ours was an ordinary existence. But two events changed our lives forever. These events took the complexity of our family dynamics to a whole new level—we would never be the same again. At the time, I did not know just how much these two events would impact my life.

. . .

If ever a child possessed star quality, it was my sister. When it came to good looks and a quick mind, it seemed Janie could upstage Shirley Temple, the immensely popular child star of the 1930s who went on to become a long-time diplomat. Just what Janie might have become, we'll never know. One autumn day in 1949, when she was 5 years old, things began to go terribly wrong. Because I was only 3 years old at the time, my parents told me the story when I was old enough to understand, but the details of that story have become permanently etched into my mind. Despite not being able to comprehend the gravity of what happened at the time it took place, when I was old enough, I became profoundly aware of her diminished state. When I finally did understand the gravity of her situation, I was overwhelmed by her plight and felt great compassion and love towards my sister. This compassion has stayed with me throughout my life, and has helped me deal with my own challenges and heartbreak.

All of a sudden, Janie became ill—so ill she had to be hospitalized. For a day and a half, our family's longtime physician, Doctor Lasater, perplexed by her condition, tried to determine if she had pneumonia, encephalitis, or perhaps both.

Finally, the gray-haired physician decided he should consult with someone who had specialized training. Because there was no such specialist in our small north Texas town, he contacted one in Fort Worth, about an hour's drive to the east.

An ominous darkness overtook the October sky by the time the so-called specialist arrived at Janie's bedside. The horrors he instilled upon our family that fateful night—Halloween night—were more hideous than anything Hollywood could have invented. Noting the unusual sugar content in Janie's blood, the doctor announced that she was suffering from acute sugar diabetes, a surprising diagnosis since no one in our family had ever had the disease. Undaunted by this information or by Dr. Lasater's almost two days of wrestling to reach a diagnosis, he immediately ordered a large dose of insulin. Dr. Lasater, at his wit's end, deferred to the judgment of the specialist.

Within a matter of minutes, my sister was transformed from a beautiful, bright, and vivacious child into a twisted, suffering invalid—a total and absolute shell of her former self. Since Janie's blood sugar abnormality turned out to be low threshold—the very antithesis of sugar diabetes—the last thing she needed was insulin. Janie was taken to the hospital, and by the next day, she was in what many would describe as a vegetative state. However, our family refused to think of her in such terms. No vegetable ever suffered like Janie did and no vegetable ever evoked so much love and pity.

Because Janie had been quite ill before receiving the insulin, there is no way to know for sure if she would have recovered to live a normal life had that monstrous blunder not been committed. What is all too well known to those of us who loved her is the tragic nature of her existence throughout the rest of her life.

The two doctors predicted that Janie would not live more than two years, if by some miracle she managed to leave the hospital alive. How unfair it was to my parents that the doctors just went about their lives as though their actions were perfectly excusable. In 1949, doctors were pretty much given a free pass on any action, no matter how devastating. The only solace we got was that Janie outlived them both. My parents never seriously considered suing for malpractice. My father said they had no desire to profit financially from Janie's tragedy.

As I matured and understood what had happened, the impact of Janie's illness on my life continued to grow. Often, I would go into her room to talk to her, stroke her forehead and hair and touch her arm or tummy. I made a point of talking to her with as much affection and cheer in my voice as I could. Almost without exception, doing this would elicit laughter and visible pleasure in Janie. Although I never thought of it in this way at the time, her response was similar to that of an animal such as a family dog, receiving abundant verbal and physical stroking. These interactions with my sister taught me to use my voice to attract and convince others, a skill that I honed and would use repeatedly as an adult. My relationship with my sister would also help me cope with my own devastating disease.

. . .

About the time I began to fully comprehend the horrors of Janie's condition, it became more and more clear that I too had a serious disability. The last thing I wanted for my parents was to be another source of regret and heartbreak. Throughout the years to come, my goal of making them proud through my personal achievements was never far from my mind. My goal was intensified by an awareness of the unfairness they had to cope with, and the fact they were dealt an emotional double whammy.

I never remember my parents exhibiting anything else but extraordinary character: they persevered, showed compassion, and remained almost continuously upbeat. Working in shifts, they followed a round-the-clock caregiving regimen 365 days a year. Because of the relentless attention of my parents, Janie lived another 31 years.

Making this unexpected longevity possible required many sacrifices. Mama remained within constant earshot of Janie all day, every day, lest one of my sister's convulsions go unattended. Only she alone could perform the acrobatic feat required to feed Janie, brush her teeth, and administer her medicine. In addition to changing Janie's diapers and bathing her, Mama had to give her frequent enemas, a chore made necessary by the youngster's inability to exercise. Any systematic movement of Janie's rigid limbs had to be done for her.

Besides caring for Janie, Mama laundered two to three times the normal amount for a family of five. Preparing meals meant cooking three ordinary family meals plus three very specific ones for Janie—every day. Janie's meals included little or nothing the rest of us ate. She was fed while lying flat on her back, and was unable to chew her food. For that reason, most of what she ate amounted to mush soaked in enough milk to wash it down. Somehow, Mama made it work—so much so that we all became accustomed to the sound of Janie choking and coughing. Janie would spit out the liquid, usually milk, and Mama would catch it with a spoon and put it back in Janie's mouth. The task of feeding her always fell to Mama, as she was the only one who could do it.

The stream of dishes was virtually endless, and we didn't have an automatic dishwasher. Often, my father would wash the supper dishes while mother fed Janie, and on rare occasion, Jimmy or I would help. When Mama did find a spare second, she would check on Jimmy and me. Jimmy and I simply accepted that our parents had limited time for us and limited freedom to engage with us outside the house. I quickly learned that I was not to make noise or presume on my parents' time. Jimmy and I played together and with neighboring kids, and mostly tried to stay out of the way. This was the only normal I knew while growing up—we didn't know any other existence so we never felt cheated.

My mother's time away from Janie totaled no more than a few hours per week. Most of that was spent accompanying Jimmy and me to Sunday school and church while my father watched Janie. Occasionally, a neighbor or relative would relieve Mama long enough for a trip to the Piggly Wiggly to buy groceries. When Jimmy was old enough and capable of watching Janie, Mama was able to run errands or even attend a weekly piano lesson. But Janie was never far from her thoughts.

My father worked six days a week running a small plumbing business with his uncle, and spent any free time caring for Janie. Every single day, he would come home for lunch, wash up, and move Janie from her hospital-style daybed to the special chair he designed and built for her. This device, a kind of half chair and half bed, allowed Janie a form of independent sitting, a much needed alternative to her mattress. Side rails were an essential safety feature of this chair, which was also equipped with an adjustable back, allowing its slope to be varied. From her chair at one end of the kitchen table, Janie could see and hear everything that took place as we ate meals; she could be part of the family. Almost everything our family did was centered on Janie's care, but Jimmy and I understood that that was the way things were, and would continue to be for the foreseeable future. I accepted the circumstances without giving them too much thought. Because Jimmy had been older when Janie first got sick, he didn't assimilate as well as I did, and perhaps had a harder time accepting our parents' devotion to Janie.

...

Every night, my father would call home for a short list of groceries to pick up on his way home from work. Once in the door, he would repeat his lunchtime ritual for getting Janie in her special chair at the corner of the dinner table. After supper, and for the balance of the evening, Daddy would hold his skeleton-like daughter in his lap—Janie never grew to much more than 65 pounds—and rock her while reaching around her on both sides to hold the evening paper. In an hour or two, when he had devoured the paper's contents, he would watch television. Shortly before bedtime, he would return Janie to her daybed, where Mama would give her a snack, usually warm milk. Finally, he would put her to bed for the night—in his bed.

By sleeping next to her, he was guaranteed to get wet at some point during the night when she urinated. Immediately, my father would jump up and change Janie's diaper, the diapers covering the rubber pad beneath her, and often his own bedclothes as well. He did this even on the coldest of nights while Mama slept nearby in the room's third bed. This arrangement afforded her the sleep necessary to face the new day.

There can be little doubt that Janie's illness had a deep impact on my parents' relationship. While obviously embracing responsibility for Janie's care as well as the family's well-being, their level of emotional intimacy was far less discernible to us kids. There was surprisingly little unsettling about their daily interactions. Each of them was a product of the Great Depression and both were from humble backgrounds. My father postponed marriage until he had acquired a rural tract, arranged for a small house to be constructed on it, and bought a new Chevy coupe—all paid for in cash. In addition, he managed to fund a nest egg. My mother was 20 years old, tall at 5 feet 9 inches, model-thin, brunette, and possessed a cover girl complexion. She was gifted with virtually total recall but lacked reasoning skills. By contrast, Daddy was wiry and bald, but his intellect and personality were no doubt attractive to my mother. Together, they shared a strong desire to start a family as soon as possible, and exactly nine months and nine days after they married, my brother Jimmy made his debut.

Jimmy told me he recalled overhearing our parents arguing fervently during the early years of Janie's illness, but I have no such memories. In fact, I rarely felt any tension between them. They were just always focused first on Janie's needs. By contrast, my own relationship with each of them could be turbulent and even violent at times. Mama favored Jimmy—she considered him the "good" child. To her, good meant dependent, quiet, and calm. She felt the need to show me who was boss by whipping me while saying something like, "You just do it because I said so." I never once remember her correcting, let alone spanking, Jimmy, but when it came to me, she preferred physical force to reason. On the other hand, my father would usually ask me to do tasks with a measure of respect, but he also had his limits. I was always fearful of doing something that would set him off. Showing up at the dinner table with hands that were not thoroughly clean or allowing a screen door to slam shut and potentially frighten Janie could result in a very hard slap on the side of my head. If Mama and I were a bad fit, Daddy and Jimmy were worse. Extremely slow to act, and displaying acute symptoms of what we now recognize as Attention Deficit Disorder, Jimmy was quickly dubbed "Goober" by my father. By his own admission in later life, he confessed to being impatient. My father could be very insensitive toward certain people while remaining monumentally empathetic toward Janie. In my judgment, Daddy devastated Jimmy's self-esteem. Perhaps that is why Mama was so protective of him. My father believed heredity determined everything. In Jimmy, he saw a behavioral tendency he had observed and disliked in both Mama and her father.

My father saw no point in trying to reshape a tendency that was in someone's genes. From my perspective, Jimmy defended himself emotionally by developing a passive-aggressive personality—at least toward Daddy. My father, in turn, came to regard Jimmy as someone who sleepwalked through life, always looking for the path of least resistance. He saw me as energetic, spontaneous, and even a fractious version of himself. The big challenge for me with both Mama and Daddy as a small child was trying to keep out of trouble. As a result, Jimmy and I both became cautious and guarded, which was obvious when we tried to relate to people at our church—people who just wanted to help. We became known for being introverted

Because we needed to remain quiet at home, most of my pleasant childhood memories are of activities which took place outside our house—even the sound of a screen door closing could trigger one of Janie's violent convulsions. As a result, our house was not a very good place for an energetic preschooler like me.

Our next-door neighbor, a spirited older woman we called Izzi, provided a sanctuary of sorts. Izzi never seemed to tire of having kids underfoot, whether in her living room, kitchen, front porch, or in her backyard. Her house sat squarely between ours and Larry's and Joe's, best friends to Jimmy and me. The four of us spent countless hours fending off imaginary Indians from the heights of the giant chinaberry trees or from atop an old tin shed strategically located in Izzi's backyard. Even though we all had huge backyards, we were never told to be quiet when we were in Izzi's yard. We could yell and scream as much as we wanted.

. . .

I spent very little one-on-one time with Mama during the worst years of Janie's sickness. However, on my fourth birthday, we did enjoy some time together—without Janie or even Jimmy. I remember swinging in an enclosed swing, and how overprotective Mama was, afraid I would somehow fall to the ground and suffer some terrible fate as Janie had. Like everything else about that afternoon, the weather was perfect. For an unforgettable couple of hours, life was idyllic. For the first time, I imagined this was how life must be for "normal" families.

In August of 1952, my parents took Janie to Houston to see a highly esteemed medical doctor. I spent the week they were gone with my grandparents, and had never experienced the amount of time and attention they devoted to me. Grandmamma and Granddaddy Haning lived in a four-room stucco farmhouse with no indoor toilet and only a cold-water sink in the kitchen. There was no telephone, television, or air conditioning. Granny cooked over a wood-burning stove, the house's source of heat during winter along with a pot-bellied wood-burning stove. Granddaddy was 6 feet tall and 180 pounds; year-round, he wore coveralls and a long sleeve shirt. He insisted his wardrobe choice kept him cool in summer and warm in the winter. Granny was also tall and was what we referred to as big-boned, but her red hair and fair skin was a contrast to Granddaddy's dark complexion. Granny wore dresses made from flour sacks, a nod to having survived the Great Depression and Dust Bowl. My grandparents lived on a small farm where they produced almost everything they consumed. Nothing meant more to me than the hours my grandparents spent playing with me on the cement floor of their screened-in porch and teaching me how to milk cows and gather eggs. My grandparents loved me unconditionally.

Even though I reveled in the attention my grandparents gave me, after about a week, I grew eager and even anxious for my parents' return.

My excitement at seeing my parents was heightened further when they showed up in a brand new 1952 Chevrolet sedan. They had left in a 1941 coupe. As I entertained myself by checking out this new set of wheels during the hour-long drive home, I had no awareness of the symbolism around me. We were moving toward a brand new era in Janie's life, an era in which her terrible seizures and our family's empathetic grimacing would become less intense and less frequent. Mercifully, the Houston physician prescribed a drug which helped control the violent, ever-present convulsions which had characterized the previous three years of Janie's illness. From that point on, her symptoms seemed to improve, ever so gradually, with the passing of each year. For our family, this would be a far more wonderful surprise than what I had felt upon seeing our first new car.

This trip held yet another symbol: a second round of heartache. Neither I, nor anyone around me, had a clue that anything was wrong. That would soon change.

The personal tragedy I was about to experience would have seemed devastating in any other family. But compared to Janie's plight, it somehow didn't seem so devastating.

By the time my personal tragedy began to unfold, I was 6 years old and entering first grade. For three years, I had increasingly come to understand the gravity of Janie's situation. Because of a desire to encourage Janie's spirit, to communicate with and nourish that one faculty which endured—her capacity to receive love—I showered her with physical and verbal affection. The reciprocal impact of that outpouring, coupled with a growing desire to bless my parents, whom I realized were now dealing with not one, but two heartbreaks, would motivate me to deal effectively with my own disability. The love I would develop for that precious, helpless person exerted a powerful and unique influence on me—by giving me the heart I needed to cope and eventually to flourish in my lifelong struggle ahead.

CHAPTER 2

THE FOG ROLLS IN

When I was in first grade, at the urging of my teacher, my parents took me to see an ophthalmologist in Fort Worth. Mama and Janie would remain in the car while Daddy and I saw the doctor.

That trip proved a waste of both time and money, because the doctor insisted that there was nothing wrong with my eyesight. His diagnosis was simple: I simply didn't know the alphabet, and for that reason alone was unable to read the eye chart at the far end of the room.

I didn't understand the purpose for all of this, even though I did realize that my teacher's note to my parents had been the impetus. Because my loss of sight had occurred gradually and at such an early age, I had no real sense that anything was wrong. I was simply being a good son, and speaking only when asked a direct question. There was no sense of disappointment at receiving no remedy because I didn't realize I was going blind. I just remember how long the room was and how strange it had been to look out the window from so high up—I had never been in such a tall building. Not only did the doctor dispute my claim of knowing the alphabet, he dismissed my father as well. Immediately, I knew there was something wrong with this doctor's behavior—something inappropriate. Although I lacked the words and the assertiveness to say anything, I resented his attitude towards me and my father.

Apparently, the doctor was looking for either nearsightedness or farsightedness, and neither was present at this point (it would show up later). Perhaps if the nearsightedness that eventually surfaced had been present then the doctor might have discovered the truth—that I was losing my sight. Any effort to fit me with glasses to produce normal vision would have been a total failure.

That physician's arrogance at dismissing both my father's statements and my teacher's observations was the first of many such hurdles I would have to cross during my lifetime.

For someone like me—legally, but not totally blind—the world appears encased in a blanket of fog. I could see an object such as a building, automobile, baseball, or printed page much the same as any other child, but I had to be 40 to 50 times closer to whatever it was I was looking at. The larger the object and the greater the contrast of colors, the farther I can see it. For example, I can count the windows in the side of a building from 100 feet or farther; determining a person's eye color might not be possible from a distance of two or three feet. Because my daily activities prior to attending school involved larger objects and because I had become so adept at moving closer to see and interact with others without standing out, my sight impairment had only now become apparent.

Looking back on that day, it seems so incredible that someone enjoying the income and status of a medical doctor could have been so unimaginative and closed-minded. He failed to think of the obvious: handing me something to hold in my hand or having me walk toward the chart. How ironic it was that this eye doctor was blind to what was wrong with me. There was, however, one bright spot to his ineptness: Even if he had diagnosed my condition properly, he would have been powerless to correct the impairment. As we would learn years later, the disorder known as optic atrophy is not treatable.

The next day, I returned to school without help, without the expectation of getting help, and without even realizing I needed help. Of course, I gave little thought to being disappointed because from my perspective, nothing had really changed. Instead, I simply returned to life with the only vision I had ever known. Although doctors would later speculate about when my once normal vision had begun to deteriorate, the disease had both begun and completed its destructive work before I ever attempted to read or write. The emotional impact of discovering how different I was and of the bitterness of my struggles and humiliations unfolded from one circumstance to another— on a kind of time-release basis. My father had an expression that captured the essence of my experiences over the next two decades: "You have two strikes against you." Like Babe Ruth, I struck out more than 1,000 times. Unlike

Babe Ruth, it took me that long to start hitting home runs. Thankfully, my father lived to see, and rejoice in, many of my achievements.

We are just beginning to determine what causes optic atrophy, but it seems to manifest itself in two forms: one hereditary, one not. With each form, a seemingly healthy optic nerve begins to deteriorate during early childhood. The duration of the atrophy and thus the extent of sight loss varies dramatically from child to child. The congenital variety is typically less severe than its counterpart. In my case, roughly 98 percent of the optic nerve's functioning was destroyed in each eye before the devastation finally ceased—and before we even realized what had happened. While I was engaged in typical preschool activities, my sight loss was not particularly noticeable to those around me. That fact, coupled with my parents being distracted by caring for Janie, resulted in no one realizing there was even an issue until I was in first grade.

In order to function, I needed to slump over my desk all day at a distance of two or three inches from my textbooks and Big Chief notebook. Even then, my efforts produced lackluster results. The most embarrassing consequence of my sight impairment came when it was necessary for me to read material written on the chalkboard. I would have to get out of my seat and walk to the chalkboard in front of the room. Then I would have to walk up and down, back and forth, in front of the chalkboard. I could see only what was, literally, right in front of me. Needless to say, this interfered with the ability of the other kids to see the contents of the board, which only made me more self-conscious—and humiliated. Returning alternately to my desk and then the chalkboard, each time I reached my desk, I tried to remember as much of the board's contents as possible so as to reduce the number of embarrassing trips and end my misery. My memory was exceptional and was a skill I continued to nurture throughout my life to make up for my poor eyesight.

Most kids want to fit in, and I was no exception. Showcasing my disability was the very last thing in the world that I wanted. For me, it was the emotional equivalent of having to stand in front of the room naked. I don't remember discussing this with my parents, but from time-to-time I did share with them my concern for what the other kids might think or say. Their response was always the same. They would assure me that there was no reason for me to be ashamed because nobody should think less of me because of my sight limitation. Unfortunately, kids can be cruel—especially some kids. I realize now that some of my teachers arranged to have the most nurturing kids sitting around me, mostly girls, as I recall.

Life on the playground was more humiliating. I was almost always the last one chosen for a team during our daily recess. There was no choice but to endure this daily dig—every single day of every school year. Knowing that my teammates wished I were not on their team was certainly unpleasant, but I used the one resource I possessed for coping: what I might do to redeem myself or at least minimize the embarrassment.

Once a team captain, always one of the best players, was stuck with me, he would relegate me to the outfield, where there would presumably be fewer occasions for me to catch, or more often, not catch the ball. Any time I heard the crack of a bat, butterflies stirred inside me. I just hoped and prayed the ball was heading toward somebody else; anybody else but me. If not, my teammates began screaming my name and hollering over one another to guide my actions. At this point, I knew I was in trouble. My worst fear was a fly ball coming straight at me. The knowledge that I might be hit with the ball before seeing it was less a concern than fear of missing what should have been an easy catch, providing the other team with a home run. The best-case scenario was a ground ball coming toward me at a slow pace, because I could trap the ball and throw it to an infielder. Of course, that presented a dilemma all its own: Should I throw to first or second base? I knew the general direction of first and second base and could tell there was someone or something standing on or near each spot. Presumably, the person at whose direction I was aiming was looking my way, but I couldn't tell.

Being nearly blind did not keep me from having a good arm and a surprisingly good aim. These gifts became apparent one afternoon as Jimmy and I waited for the school bus. Two brothers, the biggest boys in sixth grade and both bullies, began chunking rocks at Jimmy. I was a few feet away and realized what was going on. Just as Jimmy began to return fire, I picked up a rock and hit the larger of the two right in the forehead. I'm sure if I had been able to see him better, I probably would have run the other way. However, the bully burst into tears, and the rock fight was abruptly over. Jimmy and I had played more with each other than with anyone else. An attack on one of us was an attack on both of us.

When batting, I never knew the identity of the pitcher by looking at him; instead, I listened to the other kids shout out his name. To me, a pitcher had no face, fingers, glove, or baseball, for that matter. What I was transfixed on was an overt movement of his throwing arm. If he decided to wind up once before launching the ball, I usually swung before the ball ever left his glove. The ball leaving his hand meant nothing to me—at best, it would come into view about five or six feet before crossing the plate. There was no time to adjust the position of my body. Any adjustments had to be made with my arms, and my best view of the ball came when it was directly over the plate.

Once in a while I would hit a home run when we played baseball. Curiously, it was experiences like those precious few home runs and equally rare moments of academic recognition, none of which I experienced during grade school, that would help me develop what I call a *scientific temperament*. I was willing to fail hundreds or even thousands of times if necessary in order to taste the exhilarating flavor of exceptional achievement—it was what drove me during those days. Thomas Edison knew this spirit when he said, "Genius is 10 percent inspiration and 90 percent perspiration." Quite possibly, Edison's famous "never say die" attitude toward invention was an outgrowth of his coping with a severe hearing impairment since late childhood. By the time he received his first patent, he had had two decades of experience with persevering, problem solving, and persevering some more.

My own *scientific temperament* would be composed of two elements: perseverance and optimism. Like physically impaired children everywhere, I would have to invest far more than others in life. It wasn't good or bad—that's just the way it was. In my case, there was never any doubt; I was willing to make the investment. My father described me as having "a world of determination." To make up for my lack of sight, I had enough self-confidence to not allow myself to be bullied by unfortunate circumstances. In order to survive, I used every bit of physical and mental energy I possessed to push back any negativity. Virtually all responsibility for dealing with obstacles was left to me, so I had no choice but to quickly learn how to solve my problems on my own. Not because I wanted to, but because I had no choice.

While there were many elements that combined to give me a strong sense of self-confidence, the development of a *scientific temperament* was my foundation. To be sure, it wasn't easy and would take years. Even with my lousy sight, I managed to play well with other kids. Whether tossing a football in the front yard, shooting BB guns, or riding horses, I was always game, and even good at some of these activities.

Elementary school had a profound effect on how I would adjust to losing most of my sight. Mrs. Sanders, the person who prompted our trip to the ophthalmologist, helped me make the best of the situation without creating a fuss about it. She taught me to read, no small accomplishment. Not only did my severely limited eyesight require me to bury my face in the primers to see the print, there was an additional drawback at work, as we would learn decades later. My particular optic nerve disorder dramatically slows the flow of information from the eye to the brain. Consequently, I would have to look at a word or even a letter for several seconds before my brain got the information. Ironically, my reading speed might have been no greater even if the print size had been doubled.

The introduction of arithmetic, with its emphasis on adding or subtracting one numeral from or to another, was better suited to my circumstances. The need to memorize multiplication tables or the spellings of 25 words each week were relatively easy tasks because they didn't require reading—at least not rapid reading.

By third grade, I had become severely nearsighted, also known as myopic, and what a blessing it was because I had no possibility of doing schoolwork without getting extremely close to the material. Two years had passed since my trip to the ophthalmologist, and my parents decided to take me to a local optometrist to see if he might be able to help me. He was indeed able to fit me with glasses that made my "walking around" vision brighter and improved my ability to see objects a little better, and every little bit was important. Unfortunately, viewing anything at a distance of 14 inches or closer made using the glasses more of a hindrance than a help. Also unfortunate, the need to juggle the glasses—off for close work and on for the playground activities—was not suited for a third grader. Trying to store and keep up with glasses in a shirt pocket or on my desk was a hassle, and I worried about breaking them. Some kids made fun of me, calling me four-eyes. About the time I started wearing the glasses, one girl in my class, who was bigger than I, began harassing me. She liked to push and even hit me when the teacher was out of the room or as we were on the way out to recess. Because I was taught to never hit a girl, I put up with the nonsense longer than I should have. Finally, I had endured enough and popped her in the nose. She ran off crying and told the teacher I had hit her. Much to the girl's chagrin, she got no sympathy and the teacher, who had figured out long ago what was going on, never said a word to me. From that day on, third grade was a lot more pleasant. At some point, I decided the glasses were more trouble than they were worth, and they soon landed in a drawer at home.

By fourth grade, my terrible eyesight became even more of an issue than it had been before, as the print size in textbooks shrank significantly. To make matters worse, we did frequent drills in using the dictionary. My teacher, Mrs. Bean, never made me feel like a failure because I could not work as fast as the other kids. Each day after lunch, she would read a story aloud. For once, my ability to listen rather than see was the skill that counted. Listening, unlike looking, was relaxing and the stories captured my imagination. They also allowed me to perceive the value of learning to read well. The personal warmth and teaching skill, coupled with my acute nearsightedness, allowed me to make the difficult transition to the small print that would impede me from that time forward.

By this time, I had learned to rely almost entirely on tonal inflection except when interacting with someone at a distance of no more than three or four feet. And I perceived warmth and encouragement from Mrs. Bean. She made intolerable circumstances tolerable and helped me make perhaps the most difficult transition I would face in public school. On the first day of fourth grade, the world of textbooks grew forever more distant for me. From that point on, the print would be so much smaller that reading became almost impossible. Tackling a single page of reading was a major undertaking. Not only was it dreadfully slow and awkward, it was painful—literally and figuratively. The strain of holding my head scarcely above the surface of my desk all day was intensified. Because the print was so much smaller, it was no longer possible for me to keep my head in the middle of the page and move my eyes from left to right. I now had to move my head around a lot more in order to keep the print as close as possible to my eyes. Especially onerous was the requirement that I look up words in a dictionary, with its even tinier print. Had I not, by this time, become severely myopic the task would have been impossible.

It was in fourth grade that I became acutely aware of the grading system. My new sense of being graded pitted me against myself more than against others. While I knew that many other students made better grades, I was focused on trying to earn Cs and avoid making Us, because Us stood for *unsatisfactory*. I understood all too well that Cs were passing and Us were failing. At this point in my life, I was focused on measuring up to my parents' expectations and to a lesser extent, my teachers'. Because my parents understood the difficulties I faced in school, they were happy as long as I earned passing grades. Moreover, Jimmy's academic performance was worse than mine, and he had no vision impairment.

By the fifth grade I had dealt with so many intimidating situations it dawned on me that I could endure and work around or through any obstacle, but still hated to be embarrassed. In fifth grade, a trip to the zoo had a deep impact on me. While most kids would have enjoyed the trip, for me it was magical—it was the one day throughout all of elementary school when I felt most nearly like just another kid. For once, the other kids and I were all looking in the same direction, staring at the same wonders instead of the other kids looking at me, waiting for me to embarrass myself again. Nothing we did forced me to stick my face in dried ink, stand in front of a chalkboard, or miss a fly ball that virtually hit my glove. The first things I noticed were the gigantic trees. Many of the animals were huge, and the cages were generally shallow, permitting me to see the animals at close range. It was almost as though the whole place had been designed with me in mind.

Toward the end of fifth grade, I was sent to "the barracks," where I was given a test by a woman I didn't know. That was my first and only trip to that strange looking structure where the kids went who were not smart enough to attend class with everybody else. The woman administering the test was very friendly. It was the first time a teacher ever gave me a test where I was the only student in the room and where she read all the questions aloud and then wrote down my answers. This went on for about two to three hours or more, but I didn't mind. This was a lot easier than my customary classroom duties, and she seemed pleased with my answers. I was doing just fine on her test and I knew it.

After the test, no discernible changes were implemented and nothing whatsoever was said to my parents. I realize now, of course, that the test was given to determine if I was mentally disabled—retarded was the term used at the time. The possibility of my being gifted was probably never considered. IQ tests often underestimate the abilities of persons with impairments—especially

17

children—sometimes by a grotesque margin. Unfortunately, physical impairments can sometimes be mistaken for mental ones.

In the sixth grade I was larger than my tiny teacher, Mrs. Bryant, and no doubt considerably stronger. After snooping around in the classroom closet with a buddy, I realized there was an opening in the ceiling that led to the attic. Any time Mrs. Bryant would leave the room, we would hurry to the closet and pull ourselves up into the attic and begin crawling across its floor, directly above our classroom. Naturally, this was dangerous, since that floor was also the ceiling. One move and we could have plunged 12 feet or more. After we had repeated this procedure several times, the inevitable happened, and we got caught. She took me out in the hall and talked to me. She did not punish me or send me to the principal's office as I expected. Instead, she reasoned with me, and I immediately developed a deep sense of respect for her. Never before had I been corrected in a manner like that, a manner which preserved my dignity. Suddenly, I became motivated to please her, or, at the very minimum, to never disappoint her again.

. . .

During the summer between grade school and junior high, one of the most wonderful things that could ever happen to a 12-year-old boy happened to me. My parents bought me a motorbike. What amazes me most is not that Dad had the insight and courage to do that for me but that he convinced my ever-fearful, often overprotective mother to go along with it. For both my parents the motorbike was a gamble, but it was a gamble that paid off. Dad realized what was ahead for me—life without a car. All the other boys would be getting their drivers' licenses and buying cars—but not me. Years later, he reflected on this decision and remembered how he had come to realize that I "had to have something." Since we lived out in the country, there were plenty of dirt roads for me to ride on without getting on pavement. What few cars I encountered on these roads were traveling at a snail's pace and were kicking up a cloud of dust that made them easier to see.

Their decision was no doubt influenced by the fact that for several years, I had been crossing city streets and even the highway in front of our house without incident. However, what they had not understood was the role that listening had played—especially when crossing the highway. Being able to see a car coming toward me in town at a speed of 30 miles per hour or less was one thing. The 100 feet or so at which I could see an automobile was adequate in town but not when facing high-speed traffic on the highway. One evening soon after I got the bike, we were out in the front yard watching our neighbor constructing a new home directly across the highway from us, and I was sitting on my scooter. My father expressed plans to walk over there and told me I could ride my scooter. Unable to hear the highway traffic because of the engine noise, I came within a second of pulling out in front of a speeding Plymouth, which I was able to identify when it was within a few feet from me. This experience terrified me almost as much as it did my parents. After that, I was confined to riding in the borrow ditch, land from adjacent property owners "borrowed" from the local government to construct a ditch that would direct water off the roadway. The borrow ditch led down to the little country store, where it provided access to a dirt road that I could use without worrying about traffic.

Whether dirt or gravel, these rural roads had one important character-istic in common. A pair of ruts divided each into thirds. By driving strictly in the rightmost lane, I could stay out of the way of oncoming automobiles. Thus, it was not essential for me to see these cars, although I typically man-aged to do so perhaps 30 to 40 seconds before encountering them. Another factor that made it possible for me to function was contrast. The bland backdrop of sand or gravel permitted a sharp contrast to the colored auto-mobiles. The importance of contrast in helping me function could hardly be overstated. For example, if there was nothing but blue sky to serve as a backdrop, I could see a football and even a baseball well enough to play catch. By carefully choosing just the right spot, I could make this work. Sadly, such was never possible on the playground at school but was at home. If a ball crossed in front of a tree or house on its way, it was liable to hit me in the face before I saw it.

About the same time I got the motorbike, my father gave me a new .22-caliber rifle and let me start hunting with it and a .410 shotgun. Soon I became skilled at shooting birds against the background of a blue sky, and with the use of a small scope on the rifle could hit objects such as branches floating on the blue surface of the nearby Brazos River. Jimmy, who was already a crack shot, taught me the basics and often included me on expeditions where these skills could be put to good use.

Riding that scooter did much more than provide me countless hours of fun—it strengthened my conviction that I could do almost anything and helped my self-confidence. I'm sure that's the part of the reasoning behind my father's insistence on my having it. The motorbike and rifles were just a continuation of his practice of treating me as though I had no disability. He wanted to emphasize the many ways in which I was normal and de-emphasize my limitations. Many years later, he told me, "I realized you wouldn't be able to accomplish anything in life without self-confidence".

There was always a lot of work to do—it wasn't just motorbiking and shooting. Maintaining our enormous yard was like caring for two or three typical city lots. Since my father made a point of treating me as though I had normal eyesight, to the greatest extent possible, I had been mowing since I was 6. Mowing proved a blessing by giving me another opportunity to participate in life while allowing me to accomplish something of tangible benefit. Where most kids would fight with their parents about household chores, I used them as an opportunity to demonstrate to everyone—including myself—that my poor vision would not prevent me from living a normal life.

About this time, I also began to have more opportunities to work with my father in his business. This was enormously satisfying to me. Like most boys, I suppose, my father was the central person in my life and someone to emulate. Just being involved with him in an important activity was very special. Like a lot of sons, I tried hard to please my father. He was always powerful with words. He used this gift to great advantage—my own as well as his. By praising my aggressiveness and hard work, he reinforced these traits, which would prove so essential in helping me cope with my continuing struggles.

CHAPTER 3

BEING ROOSTER

As far back as I can remember, my father had a penchant for disseminating nicknames. Since Jimmy had been cursed with the degrading title of "Goober," I considered myself lucky to be summoned with a shout of "Rooster" or "Cotton," both handles I understood as references to my cotton-white hair and ever-present rooster tail, known in more formal circles as a cowlick. These affectionate terms would be replaced during my junior high years by "Fatchie," perhaps because my hair was taking on more of a brown tint and because I was wearing it in a flat top, the choice for most boys and young men in 1958. The flat top featured extremely short hair except in the front, where a gooey substance, called Butch Wax, was used to glue the front-most inch or so to stand absolutely vertical. I had no idea what a "Fatchie" was and was not sure I wanted to know—so I never asked. Some 40 years later, my father told me he had observed in me a take-charge attitude that led me to attack every obstacle with a plan and with complete determination to succeed. He was reminded of the Supreme Commander of the Allied Forces during World War I, General Ferdinand Foch, so he decided to call me Fatchie.

If I had not earned the rank of general by conquering elementary school, my performance in junior high certainly merited such a rank.

There is something very difficult about dwelling in the limbo-land of junior high, suspended dead-center between childhood and adulthood. The first several days of the seventh grade were frightening. For the first time I had multiple teachers who needed to be told about my disability. This had been hard enough when I had to explain my circumstances to one teacher per year. To make matters worse, I had become so self-conscious that I avoided explaining my circumstances. Having learned not to impose on my parents, the notion of imposing on six or seven adults scared me to death. By the time I reached junior high, the lesson I had learned so well at home was thoroughly ingrained in my psyche. My parents' responsibilities with Janie meant I was to make very few demands on them, and this message carried over to the adults I encountered at school.

On the first or second day, my teacher, Coach McQuary, instructed us to open our textbooks and take turns reading aloud. He told the person sitting at the front left side of the room to begin. I remember hoping desperately that the period would end before it became my turn. Each time someone finished and someone else began, I felt more and more apprehensive, and my stomach was in knots. When it was finally my turn, I was forced to try to explain my circumstances—with the whole class not only able to hear but focus on my every word.

There was something else strangely new and perhaps equally frightening about what took place in science class that day. I was intimidated: I had not realized just how well many of the other kids could now read. I felt like a turtle in a race of rabbits—so much so that I felt the only thing to do was to ask to be excused from reading aloud.

In earlier years my slow, stumbling reading style was more or less matched by the efforts of the other inexperienced readers. Such was clearly no longer the case, and the smaller print exacerbated my struggle to read.

To add to my sense of being overwhelmed and outmatched, we were now studying more technical scientific terms and complicated definitions. For the first time, I couldn't simply ingest every sentence that I heard read aloud. I needed to study—to mull over some of this material, an impossible task.

I realized that if I were to succeed I would have to *want* to succeed much more than my classmates did. I would have to be prepared to work harder than any of my fellow students. I would have to be willing to put forth more effort to earn Cs than others who earned As. This realization and resolve would end up serving me well.

Coach McQuary was my first male teacher. Because the only other significant male figure in my life—my father—was prone to be as critical and demanding as loving and supportive, initially I was both leery and afraid of Coach McQuary, so I avoided explaining my circumstances to him. The task of trying to make another person—even a teacher—understand the visual limits under which I labored always resulted in limited success. Most people understand total blindness or normal eyesight but not the reality that there can be something in between. I walked and even ran without a white cane or leader dog and didn't wear dark glasses. In fact, I didn't wear glasses of any kind until later. Yet, I had to get extremely close to my books and papers to read.

Fortunately, my homeroom teacher, Mrs. Fields, who also taught me English, was there to make a difference. She was fun and had a sense of humor, something not many of my teachers possessed.

There was a boy named Pablo who sat right next to me during homeroom. Pablo was the class clown. He was witty and expressive, in speech and especially in gesture. Pretty soon I began to emulate him, and loved it. While others might have regarded what Pablo and I were doing as silly, to me it was an intellectual game—my first introduction to comic relief, a much needed and welcomed diversion. And, if I managed to make other kids laugh, I felt accepted.

I had been inspired by my father's quick wit. Throughout my entire life, a sense of humor has enabled me to get through what might otherwise have been some pretty depressing circumstances. Before Mrs. Fields and Pablo, most everything at home and at school had been stone cold serious. Learning to laugh and to make others laugh, especially a teacher, was a new and welcomed experience. Life's circumstances had forced me to be very serious, but at least now I had a new way to find occasional relief and fit in.

Thanks to Mrs. Fields and Pablo, school was kind of fun—except for math class. I couldn't see one digit of the example problems our teacher worked on the board each day. I struggled terribly to try to make out the problems in the book we used for homework. There is no telling how many problems I missed on homework and tests because I misread a number. Because I couldn't see the board, I was easily distracted—and bored. One day I got so bored with my math teacher's chatter about whatever it was that she was writing on the chalkboard that I reached under my desk and extracted a book of short stories I had gotten from the school library. I had already read it once and started over again. The print was larger than usual, the brief chapters were a size which I could handle, and the biographies were about interesting people. Perhaps more than anything else, I liked the book because I had been able to read the whole thing—from cover to cover, something I had never before accomplished and would not repeat until many years later.

Needless to say, my reading style was not inconspicuous, and sure enough, before very long the teacher spotted me. She announced that if I could see enough to read a library book, I could see enough to do math. Of course that wasn't exactly true, but, nonetheless, she made her point. I never again did that in anybody's class.

My parents decided to once again take me to see a specialist. More than six years had passed since my initial trip in the first grade. In the years since, I had been examined by a local optometrist, who had fitted me with glasses when I was in the third grade. However, for reasons which I would not understand until much later, they did not work.

I'm not sure what prompted my parents to try again to see if a big city specialist could do something for me. Perhaps it was at the insistence of the optometrist or the suggestion of my junior high principal, Mr. Wilson, who took an active interest in trying to help me. He ordered large print books and even summoned me to the auditorium one day to view text he had projected on a wall to enlarge the print. Neither of these experiments paid off. The books were huge and did not correspond with those my classmates were using. Moreover, I still had to plant my face a few inches from the materials I wanted to read, which proved impractical as the books were about two feet tall, making it very difficult for me to get as close as necessary. These books were designed for children having much better vision than I—those for whom the huge print would permit them to read at a normal distance from the page. Likewise, trying to read print projected on a wall meant I had to get so close to the wall that I came between the projector and the surface. Even though these ideas did not work out, the fact that my principal would put so much thought and effort into the matter meant a lot.

Perhaps it was just their own awareness of the increasing importance of my need to see better, but whatever spurred it, my father took off work, loaded Janie into the car and he, Mama, Janie, and I headed to Dallas for the day. Jimmy, who was by now a junior in high school, stayed behind to attend school and his after-school job at the Piggly Wiggly.

Once we arrived at our destination, we parked the car where Janie could be comfortable while my parents cared for her. We finally found a place that would afford neither too much nor too little sun and at the same time was reasonably free of loud noises.

That morning one doctor examined me and then referred us to a nearby physician for a second opinion. Fortunately, we were able to see the second doctor that afternoon. After all the tests had been completed, the verdict was pronounced: There was no hope whatsoever that I would ever be able to see any better in my lifetime. The doctor spoke to my father as if I was not in the room—or would not understand the gravity of his diagnosis: "Your son's condition is known as optic atrophy, and it will never change." He went on to say that there was nothing in the way of glasses or the like that would help. I would never be able to drive and never be able to read normally.

These words stung as nothing else ever had. My eyes teared up as I listened, although I managed to fight them back. I received the news as if someone had just informed me of the death of a loved one. The finality of it all and the sense of hopelessness was devastating. I was 13 by this time and thoroughly aware of life's hardships, disappointments, and humiliations confronting a profoundly sight-impaired person.

No child should have to hear such words and no parent should ever have to suffer that kind of tragedy. Nonetheless, since it had to be said and I had to face it sooner or later, I am thankful that I heard it with my father sitting beside me. And, I'm glad I got to hear the honest industrial-strength version.

It seems that experiences like this one where a child falls victim to a tragedy may be even more hellacious for a parent than for the child. Once the doctor finished explaining the gloomy prognosis, my father paid the bill and we left. While Daddy wrote the check, I was thinking how ironic it seemed that we had to pay a lot of money to hear such devastating news. As we made the two-hour drive back to Mineral Wells, the stinging continued. I can still picture the late afternoon sky as dusk began to fall, the particularly faint view of the freeway, of surrounding automobiles, of the buildings we passed. I was pierced by the realization that this was as good a view as I would get for the rest of my life.

At one point the comment was made that it could be so much worse—I could be like Janie. I didn't say anything. Besides, I had heard this before. It had never helped before, and this was certainly no exception. There could be little question that Janie's existence was much worse than my own. I knew that. Still, I suffered in my soul, and I damn well had a right to feel hurt and disappointed.

Jimmy, on the other hand, never had any "right" to feel disappointed. As the only non-disabled child in the family, it was unthinkable to my father that Jimmy could ever feel disappointed. I think this is a danger for families with one or more children with a disability. It is important to remember that feelings of disappointment are normal for everyone—abled or disabled. Such feelings are poignant and justified and need to be treated as such by parents.

A testimony to the resilience of kids, my grief had run its course by the next morning. I never looked back to this heartbreak again until now, and only now, because others need to know.

The next day I was diagramming sentences, playing marbles at lunch, swinging fiercely at the softball during recess, and riding my moped down the nearby dirt road after school.

Before long we would realize a modest and unexpected aftermath to our trip to Dallas. We learned about a doctor in Fort Worth who had a new device which might help me. Mama and I went over to see about it one Saturday morning while Jimmy stayed home with Janie.

Like every other doctor before him, this doctor also examined my eyes. When he finished, he turned to Mama and like the previous doctor we had visited, addressed her as if I wasn't in the room: "You need to understand that there is no way that Walter can ever complete high school." Fortunately, and for whatever reason, I didn't suffer from this pronouncement as I had from the last such doctor-patient chat. Maybe I was numb, or just angry. While these words saddened me at first, within a matter of seconds I dismissed them as one more pronouncement based on faulty precepts.

I had learned at an early age that my own ability to understand what I could do was vastly superior to other so-called experts, such as this doctor. I had lived with my disability for more than a dozen years and experimented with it countless times per day.

Editorial comments by many "authority" figures let me know that my own thoughts wouldn't be valued and certainly were not solicited or even permitted. I understood this and played the game—always polite, always quiet.

I had my own agenda: my own confidence and faith in God. There was in my spirit unshakable and irrefutable evidence of things not seen.

Pretty soon we got around to what we had come to see. My mother and I were taken into another room, where I was seated at a table right in front of a contraption, the likes of which I'd never seen before. It stood about 15 or 16 inches high, was about two feet long from front to back, and the face of it slightly resembled a modern-day microfiche monitor. Yet there were striking differences. For instance, this device was hinged at the very back so that it would open like the mouth of an alligator, only not as wide. The alligator's design made it possible to place books of various thicknesses within its jaws. The base of the unit was designed to accommodate reading material like a book or magazine. It consisted of two principal parts: a stationary platform which supported the entire machine and a sliding tray which could be moved from left to right and from front to back.

The upper portion of the machine was the actual monitor or viewer. While this upper unit contributed the majority of the total bulk, it was extremely light and simple. Beneath what, on a smaller scale, resembled the hood of a 1920s touring car, was a system of mirrors, a light, and a magnifier. All of this gadgetry cooperated to produce a substantially enlarged reproduction of the print beneath it.

This viewer could enhance normal textbook size print to roughly one-half inch or so in height. This made it much easier to see—and read. I read some sample materials in the doctor's office, and Mama decided to purchase the device right then and there. The machine cost $150, a not insignificant sum for a middle-class family in 1959—after all, my motorbike had cost $110 the previous summer. Nonetheless, she wrote the check without thinking twice, and we loaded the machine into the back of our car and started back to Mineral Wells.

After we got home, I searched out a suitable place to erect a card table near an electrical outlet and placed the viewer on it. One of the first books I placed under the viewer was my civics textbook, which I read for a half hour or more. Then, I looked at some magazines and papers. This exercise helped me to understand both the capabilities and limitations of the viewer.

Unfortunately, its limitations proved far more numerous than its capabilities: It could not be used to help me see what I was writing. It wasn't portable enough to haul to school and back each day. The screen produced a glare and had a grainy texture which made it tiring to watch. But perhaps the most serious limitation was the slowness of reading this way.

In spite of all its drawbacks, the viewer helped me develop my reading skills beyond the third grade level, where I had essentially peaked, as the print size decreased after that. It helped me with a portion of my assignments in some courses.

By the time the seventh grade was drawing to a close, the combination of a keener sense of humor, a more mature attitude toward school, and to a lesser extent, the availability of the viewer helped me earn somewhat better grades than in the past.

My improving grades was one of the factors that prompted a phone call I will never forget. That Wednesday afternoon in May of 1959 seemed just like any other afternoon. Mama had gone to town to do some shopping, so I was staying in the house where I could keep an eye on Janie. The phone rang; it was my father making his customary grocery check. As soon as I picked up the receiver and said hello, Daddy said, "Old Byron Kaziah will be along in a few minutes. He's going to bring you a new little yellow Indian motorcycle and get your old moped. Your mother and I are proud of the good work you've been doing in school, and we want you to have it."

I could hardly believe what I was hearing. Sure enough, Mama soon drove up, followed almost immediately by Mr. Kaziah. It felt a little like trading an old pair of shoes for new ones—exciting but something you needed to break in. By the time Mr. Kaziah was out of sight on my old moped, that sense of awkwardness had vanished. I was set for a summer of fun.

Within a couple of weeks, school ended. One of the very first things I did that summer was to invite my friend, Joe Neal, to come down and spend the afternoon riding that motorcycle with me.

Later on that summer, his folks bought him one just like mine, and we would get to ride together from time to time. There was no requirement that we have driver's licenses because one was not needed to drive motorbikes having less than five brake horsepower. Our bikes had been designed with this law in mind and thus were powered by 4.9 horsepower engines. They were capable of speeds of up to 55 miles per hour and, thus, could be driven on the highway. This proved especially beneficial to Joe, as his parents had moved four miles further out into the country by this time. It meant that he was independent, could ride into town, and—of even greater importance to me—come down to my house and go riding.

Because of my limited eyesight, I was restricted to riding off the pavement until later, when this restriction was, on rare occasion, lifted by special permission. I truly appreciated my parents buying me first a motorbike and then this small motorcycle. Notwithstanding that each had brought me countless hours of fun, I sometimes felt cheated. If Janie had personified all the reasons why I should feel somehow fortunate, Joe Neal personified all the reasons I felt cheated. He was everything, he had everything, and he could do everything. Joe was bright, athletic, and good-looking. Most of all, he could see.

I watched Joe ride his motorcycle to Little League practice that summer and then to football practice once school started. Each day at school I'd go out to the place where all the motorbikes and scooters were parked during lunch and wish that my bike were there for everybody to see.

I pleaded with my parents to let me ride my cycle to school, but of course they could not. I said it was so unfair for Joe to be able to do all these things while I could not. Once again, the predictable comment was made about how much better off I was than Janie. And, once again, those comments didn't comfort me. I would have rather heard something like, "Yes, I know it hurts."

. . .

On January 12, 1960, my sister, Mary Frances, was born. I was sitting in geography class listening to Mr. Burkham call out each person's grades for the semester when word came that I had a baby sister. The news that I had made a B, though a cause for pride itself, was completely overshadowed by the real news. Mary's birth was a wonderful event for the whole family.

She had come along so late that to my brother and me, she felt more like our own child than our baby sister. Mama was almost 39 and Daddy was 50.

I heard our old friend, Pastor Tom Norris, tell my father, "I told you the Lord would make it up to you about Janie." I believed then as I do now that this comment captured the intense joy of this event. However, I realized immediately that his statement was wrong. Nothing could erase the grief that we felt over Janie, and besides, if there was anyone to whom restitution was owed it was Janie herself. No event—not even this joyous one—could do that. Even so, there was more happiness and enthusiasm in our home than I had ever known, and I shared deeply in it.

With a newborn in the house and Janie to be cared for as always, my mother was busier than ever. Although it was a long, very gradual improvement in Janie's condition that had made it possible to even consider another child, she nonetheless required even more care than the infant.

During my whole eighth grade year while Mama was first pregnant and then later after Mary was born, Daddy would wash the supper dishes. At this time each night, I would put my viewer on the table and read geography aloud. Time would not permit me to read every subject, so I focused on reading geography. This allowed me to make As and Bs in this one subject, something I'd never done before. Also, it helped me improve my reading skills.

As the school year and my junior high days simultaneously drew toward a close, another blessing came my way: Our local optometrist fitted me with some glasses that helped noticeably. They took away the nearsightedness and thereby produced a much brighter view of the world. As in the third grade, these glasses had to be removed for reading (for reasons that I would not understand until years later) but my other vision was perceptibly better. This made riding my cycle a little bit safer, although extreme caution was still necessary. This was the last in a series of changes which marked this period of transition.

I left junior high a bit abler. It had given me a sense of humor and a little more self-confidence. I felt a sense of pride when I graduated. As I contemplated high school, the thought that I might not succeed was only in the minds of a few truly "blind" individuals—the thought never crossed my own mind.

CHAPTER 4

DREAM NIGHTMARE

Entering high school in the fall of 1960 marked the beginning of a new era for me—one which would see me grow from being one of the smallest boys on campus to one of the tallest. However, it was my spiritual growth that would prove to be the most dramatic. It was during this time that I began to dream. And to realize that those dreams could be realized.

My freshman math teacher was the first teacher who failed me. While I may have deserved to fail, I didn't like it. By repeating the course, I was able to achieve the highest grade in the class—the second time around. This time I realized that I had a responsibility to ask for help, help that enabled me to excel in a course that had given me so much grief earlier. I realized how important it was to advocate for myself.

During my sophomore year, I had both the worst and best experiences I would have attending public school. The fall of 1961 got off to a somewhat worse than usual start. The beginning of a school year was never pleasant for me because I had to explain my visual challenges to a new batch of teachers, and this year was no different. Every year, at least one of my teachers would suggest that I should "get glasses." I had endured that naive and irritating suggestion one too many times, and I responded with, "Now, why didn't I think of that?" This was not well received by the school's new English teacher, who had enough trouble trying to cope with an overcrowded classroom. My usual efforts to hide or at least minimize my disability proved especially unsuccessful. The teacher's response was to comment that I was "blind as a bat" behind my back. He did manage to demonstrate some concern towards me once he realized that my vision was not one easily corrected with glasses.

Shortly thereafter, a new sophomore English class was formed to address the overcrowding, and I was transferred to that class. The teacher of this new class—Mrs. Beth Downs—would turn out to be the greatest teacher I would ever have.

Mrs. Downs and the literature we studied together would contribute uniquely to the quality of my life. At last, my ability to think, to perceive, and to discern had an outlet. Always before, my performance in school had been measured in terms of my ability to read and retain information on a competitive basis with other students, all of whom could read better than me. Mrs. Downs taught me that the ability to *understand* such things as what Shakespeare meant when he used a particular symbol are what really mattered.

I felt an exhilarating sense of personal achievement while learning about the power and beauty of words. For me, hearing the words of Shakespeare and other literary giants, essentially for the first time, was like hearing a great orchestra for the first time. I was deeply moved. From that time forward, I developed a love of writing and expression.

This introduction to literature by such an inspiring teacher was for me a call to personal excellence. It caused me to see a very different personal horizon.

That same year, I had another experience which has greatly enriched my life. Curiously, my participation in this activity was one that came after a little kicking and screaming on my part.

During the previous summer, my mother had received a phone call from the principal's office. It seemed that the principal had been reviewing my degree plan and decided I needed to take "speech" during my sophomore year.

As a 15-year-old boy whose primary interests up to that point had been vocational agriculture and using pipe wrenches or posthole diggers, the idea of taking speech was abhorrent. I wanted nothing to do with it. Despite my protests, I studied speech during my sophomore year and liked it so much that I took it my junior and senior years as well. Just like Mrs. Downs' class taught me to think, speech taught me how to express myself. It transformed me in a way I had not thought possible.

To think that I could succeed as a public speaker required a certain amount of audacity, a stubbornly abundant ingredient in my character. After all, I couldn't see any material placed on the podium—that meant no notes, no papers, and no outlines. But I believed I could do it anyway—all from memory. Developing my speaking skills gave me more confidence that I could succeed—on my terms.

In my junior year, my English teacher was certainly pleasant enough, but I never felt she saw in me the type of potential I had increasingly come to see for myself—thanks to Mrs. Downs. I suspect I was in a class of students of which little was expected, including me. Mrs. Campbell never seemed to get past the stereotypical measuring sticks for assessing my true intellectual or emotional capacities. Perhaps she assumed we had little interest in learning, so she didn't put forth her best effort. On the other hand, maybe my disappointment with literature that year had more to do with the literature being taught than with the teacher.

To be sure, Mrs. Campbell lacked experience with someone like me. On the contrary, Mrs. Downs had had firsthand experience. Although I did not know it when she was teaching me, Mrs. Downs had a sister who was deaf and often presumed to be unintelligent when she was actually extraordinarily bright. There can be little doubt that this experience equipped her for her very special ministry to me. She was one of the first people who could truly empathize with me.

Mrs. Downs interpreted such factors as my terrible spelling, poor handwriting, awful scores on achievement tests (which I wasn't able to read in their entirety), and my overall academic standing as symptoms of poor eyesight instead of irrefutable evidence of my limited insight.

The tragedy is not that once upon a time a kid with poor eyesight was misjudged and underestimated in his struggle to fulfill his dreams. The real tragedy is that every class I attended for those who "weren't college material" contained many other underestimated kids. I wonder how many of these cast-offs resigned themselves to adopting an ill-conceived and prejudicial message that they should stop dreaming.

My junior-year English teacher was closer to the norm than to the exception. Teachers, especially inexperienced and insecure ones, look for someone or something (like standardized tests) to tell them what their opinion should be of a student. Unfortunately, that meant she was unable to see the real me. Strangely, I feel a sense of warmth and identity with her and those like her who are good people trying to do a job well, a job they know is important.

Such persons, though strong in many ways, also struggle against personal limitations. The teacher who develops the ability to uncover intellectual strength in a student, where it is so thoroughly camouflaged as was the case with me, is truly exceptional.

If the intellectual excitement I had enjoyed under Mrs. Downs was absent during my third year of high school, this was the year that shaped my spirit and values more than any other—before or since. The event that moved me from "lip service" to "hip service" in my walk with Christ was a very sad one. Our family's most beloved pastor, Rev. Tom Norris, died rather suddenly at the age of 66. He had been our pastor before, during, and after Janie fell ill. Throughout the 14 years between Janie's illness and when he died, he had faithfully visited our home—always speaking lovingly to Janie. He did this long after moving on to pastor elsewhere. My response was to listen to sermons at a whole new level and to rededicate my life. I was transformed from a spiritual child to a spiritual adult, albeit a less than mature one with lots of experience. As the scripture says, "all things become new." My thoughts and speech changed overnight.

Soon, I began memorizing scripture, a chapter at a time. Not long thereafter, I had a vivid dream in which I saw a beautiful young woman. She was standing at a right angle to me and had shoulder-length hair that looked white in my black and white dream, and was wearing a dress whose color matched her hair perfectly. I took this as a message from the Lord, a revelation of the person the Lord had for me—at some time in the future.

Two days after my junior year ended, my beloved Granddaddy Haning dropped dead in an instant. At the funeral, I learned that he had accepted Christ at age 17—my age at that time. When the message was over, I rushed to Mama's side to comfort her with the assurance that her father was in a better place. No sooner had I spoken these words when I realized it was Mama's younger sister I had hugged and comforted. Immediately, I felt so embarrassed and awkward. At that time, Aunt Nina was not a believer and her reaction reflected her lack of agreement. I realized my mistake; perhaps my reaction gave it away. Although my poor eyesight had caused me to endure countless awkward social experiences, this was the one I hated the most, and it made me angry.

Soon the summer got underway, my first to work full-time with Daddy. Hard work, lots of sweating, and drinking three to four gallons of water per day had rewarded me with a beautiful tan—and the first pimple-free complexion in a half-dozen years. I had saved $62, the equivalent of $400 today, and decided to go shopping on the last Saturday afternoon before school started. My first stop was at the sporting goods store, where I laid out $12 for a better scope for my .22 rifle. Next, I headed to Hoffman's department store, where I bought three short sleeve shirts for $1.99 each and two pairs of blue jeans for $3.99 each. That's everything I would need to last the next year—everything, that is, but the Future Farmers of America (FFA) corduroy jacket I'd bought earlier. A strong, secure pride and independence came over me as I walked back to Daddy's shop and called for someone to come and fetch me.

...

The very first day of my senior year, I caught enough of a glimpse of a classmate to tell that she was someone I wanted to see up close. Three days later, the opportunity presented itself during the lunch hour. As I was walking along the sidewalk in front of school, my path took a sharp turn, and there she was.

Because of my limited eyesight, I could not see her well until I was three or four feet away. Each step I took toward her improved my ability to see her as much as coming 100 feet nearer would have benefited a person with normal sight. Thus, as I walked toward her, my view of her from eight or nine feet was roughly the view that someone else would have seen from a city block. So within the span of two or three steps and two or three seconds, I went from thinking she looked very interesting to being absolutely stunned by her beauty. Her shoulder-length hair was so light in color as to appear almost white, and she was wearing a very soft yellow dress that matched the color of her hair. Almost immediately, I concluded she was the girl I had dreamed about a few months earlier. Not only was the color of her hair and dress a match, she was someone I had never known or even seen before.

I introduced myself and learned her name was Barbara Mikles, as she gave me a smile—the likes of which I had never received before. The experience was both wonderful and terrifying.

Unfortunately, I felt helpless to act. I lacked the very symbol of masculine adequacy in our culture, especially in 1963—a car. What was even more unthinkable, I lacked a driver's license. How could I ever hope to overcome this obstacle since explaining my predicament to Barbara would bring full focus on my disability—the one thing I had spent my life trying to hide from others? I concluded that I would first need to neutralize what I perceived as a huge negative before attempting to interest someone so striking. The answer seemed obvious: I would have to help her see and believe what I believed about myself—that I would eventually contribute something of value, that I would answer a high calling. If there was any chance she would ever see this, she would first have to believe I possessed exceptional intellectual abilities. I would have to apply myself to my studies as never before, and so I did.

Of course, this mammoth undertaking to win her assumed there was much more to Barbara than just surface beauty, but I was thinking that the Lord would never lead me to someone lacking the character and personality traits that would complement my own. Also, every person I had encountered from parents, to teachers, to fellow church members had been trustworthy. Besides, the girls I had known since preschool had been worthy of the respect I felt toward them. At a time when people did not bother to lock their doors or their cars and thought nothing of allowing their kids to roam about freely, I considered good character in others a given. Call me naive, but my perceptions were not that far off the mark. It was a time when virtually everyone attended Sunday school and church on a regular basis, parents talked to their children during the evening meal and over homework, and a student would volunteer to lead the whole school in a prayer carried over the loudspeaker each morning. Believing as I did that almost all girls were fundamentally good, the main differentiator for me was the level of physical attraction I felt, and when it came to Barbara, the physical attraction index was off the charts.

So, I began struggling to read at home using a magnifying glass, and managed to decipher roughly 30–40 words per minute. At that rate, there simply was not enough time at night and on weekends to read all assigned materials, so I had to be selective. The one subject that did get my full attention was literature. It was literature that both symbolized and embodied what I dreamed and aspired toward.

If I could excel in literature as I had when a sophomore, perhaps this would come to Barbara's attention. Just how this was supposed to take place, I didn't know. Maybe the new, first-year teacher of English would recognize my gifts and give me an opportunity to shine in class, the way Mrs. Downs had done. If so, I might manipulate my schedule at midterm to get in the same class with Barbara—providing me the opportunity I longed for to showcase my intellect. All this was speculative, but I was desperate and misguided. Unguided would be a better term. I was the emotional equivalent of a scud missile, knowing nothing of the value of plain straight talk. My belief that I had to first enhance my status in Barbara's eyes before attempting to initiate a relationship was pure nonsense. What I should have done is say something like this: "Barbara, I find you very attractive and a neat person and would like to get to know you better. In fact, I'd like to ask you for a date, but I have a problem: I have a sight impairment that prevents me from driving. If the idea of spending some time with me sounds appealing to you, perhaps we can find a work-around."

The same approach would have made sense as I got to know another equally beautiful and wholesome girl named Laverne Jordan. Having met Barbara a few days earlier and believing she was "The One," I was not looking for or even open to the idea of pursuing another girl. Even so, she was a second new girl in our school, a brunette who possessed jaw-dropping, breath-taking good looks that could make any healthy 17-year-old boy "slap his granny." One day in civics class, I found myself only two or three feet from her and face-to-face. As with Barbara a few days earlier, by the time I could see her clearly, I was both stunned and a bit intimidated.

Undaunted and undistracted from my strategy of trying to impress Barbara, my Herculean efforts produced only Bs and Cs and eventually As, Bs, and Cs. While these grades pleased Daddy, they were certainly not going to bring any fame to me as a student. Far more discouraging was my senior English teacher's response to me. Whereas I had hoped she would recognize my skill in discerning symbolism in the literary works we studied, that never happened. The second major exam proved instructive. My grade was 95, even though I did not miss a single question or any part of a question. She took off five points because I misspelled a word—a word unrelated to the characters or story. I was being marked down rather harshly for something I could not study to prevent.

Ironically, the intellectual gifts I was trying so hard, with zero success, to demonstrate for Barbara were on full display almost every day for Laverne.

Our civics teacher, Mrs. Hayes, got it about me. For years, Daddy had talked to me about civics and even had read newspaper articles relating to governmental affairs. For this reason, I could contribute significantly to class discussions, and it was clear to everyone in the class that I was knowledgeable on the subject and that Mrs. Hayes considered me very bright

After several months of believing my strengths had been showcased for Laverne to witness, I ran into her when she waited on me while working in a department store during the Christmas rush. As always, her personality was delightful and she was as pretty as ever. I thought, I must be crazy for not pursuing this girl. After leaving the store, I began racking my brain for some way I could ask her out. But the same old problem of transportation was still staring me in the face. This experience drove home the reality of my isolation. As a somewhat quiet and socially disengaged person, I had no good friends or sibling with whom to double date. Unlike my classmates who had grown up in town, interacting with other kids since childhood, I didn't belong to any informal group.

Once again, I lacked the gumption to communicate my feelings and give the young lady the opportunity to help me find a work-around. Only years later did I discover the principle of trusting others. I should have trusted both Barbara and Laverne to treat my expression of interest in a gracious manner— regardless of their level of romantic interest in me.

Feeling totally frustrated and thwarted in any effort to pursue Laverne, my mind turned back to pursuing Barbara. I thought that if that dream I had experienced the previous year was really a sign from the Lord, He could make something happen that was beyond my ability to foresee. As the months passed, there was absolutely no breakthrough with Barbara, and such a thing grew increasingly less likely. However, my great academic efforts were paying off. I was now determined to attend college and believed I could succeed at it—even though I lacked the most basic tools for a legally blind person considering college. Moreover, I did not even know what tools were available. No one had considered college a possibility for me and explored the tools available to help me. In point of fact, I didn't even know there was such a term as legally blind and would have never imagined such a term could apply to me.

About two months before the school year ended, I turned 18, the age at which I could apply for a driver's license without having taken drivers education. My father and I had talked about how difficult it was going to be for me to secure even the most restricted license. Our strategy was simple: I would master all the basics such as parallel parking in case I got the opportunity to take the driving portion of the test.

One morning I went to the police station before school to take the written test. Predictably, I was the last one to finish, and it became rather obvious to the examining officer that my eyesight was poor. Nonetheless, he let me finish and graded my test. There was good news and bad news. I passed the exam, but would not be allowed to take the driver's test without a letter from an eye doctor stating that he considered it safe for me to be behind the wheel of a car.

I went to see Dr. McCall, an eye, ear, nose, and throat specialist who had a practice in town.

Dr. McCall was extremely thorough and left no diopter unturned. An active member of the local school board at that very time, he put me in touch with the Vocational Rehabilitation Commission, which he did completely at his own initiative. Dr. McCall erased all hope of my getting a driver's license. In fact, he was the first expert to use the term "legally blind" to describe the extent of my disability. Believe me, it came as quite a shock to an 18-year-old who drove a motorcycle to learn that I had been blind all of my life.

The term *legally blind* was difficult for me to accept and even harder for my father to accept, as he had always believed in emphasizing the ways in which I was like other people rather than dwelling on, or magnifying, the one difference.

As is so often the case with boys, my high school years had come and gone before I developed the social skills necessary to claim the opportunities unique to that time and place.

Watching that year come to a close was particularly painful for me because I knew that my opportunity to impress and perhaps win the girl in my dream would expire on graduation day. We never did end up getting together. The cruelest irony to me lay in the fact that I became increasingly disappointed and confused about the Lord's failure, as I saw it, to make good on what I believed was a promise revealed in a dream.

When graduation day came, I would not be valedictorian or salutatorian. When the list of those receiving scholarships or belonging to the National Honor Society was read, my name was not among them, although none had pursued excellence with greater devotion.

Many accomplishments were cited that night, but the knowledge of my particular achievements was confined to the privacy of a few caring hearts. To be honest, I preferred it that way, for I was still very private about my disability. Besides, it was enough that I knew. The thought that it might be 20 years before I would see most of my classmates again never entered my mind. I didn't really care because I was ready to move on. All through high school, I had never really bonded with any of my classmates. The guys all had lives that seemed to focus around driving: part-time jobs to afford their cars, working on their cars, and taking girls on dates in their cars. My one regret about moving on was that I didn't get the girl I wanted.

My sense of the finality of it all was overpowering. The high school experience that we had shared for only the final term was expiring and with it any source of contact with Barbara. After all, it wasn't as though I could just call her up and take her to the show. As teachers lined us up in alphabetical order to enter the gymnasium/auditorium, I strained for what I understood would be my final look at Barbara, but we were too far apart for me to see her. Everything seemed so wrong—what about that dream? How could the person in that dream be anyone but Barbara? Were the timing and intricate details of that dream nothing but a very unlikely coincidence and not divinely inspired at all? Had my decision to forego any thoughts of pursuing Laverne, whose goodness and sweetness I had increasingly come to recognize through daily classroom contact, been a big mistake? There were so many questions and so few answers. There was, however, no doubt that my encounter with Barbara, as I perceived it, caused me to clarify my aspirations for life and to begin pursuing these goals with extraordinary dedication. All year, I had hoped for and prayed for just the right opportunity to share these thoughts with Barbara, in hopes that she could believe as I did about my future. Certainly, I realized that few around me would consider my vision of my future realistic. That short list would have included Mrs. Downs and Mrs. Hayes. Ironically, I think it might have included Laverne.

All hopes of sharing my goals with Barbara were now dashed, but the goals themselves were still very much alive within my spirit. At the core of these dreams was the desire to write and speak powerfully. Later, I would capture the essence of these goals as follows: "I aspired to become a sculptor of elegant and compelling thoughts both as a writer and a speaker." Without knowing it, and I dare say without even suspecting it, Barbara had a profound, important, and lasting impact on my sense of the possible. Moreover, the admiration and respect I developed for both her and Laverne has informed my attitudes and actions toward women to this very day.

Suddenly, as my time came to walk across the stage, all thoughts about the future vanished, as I nervously trusted myself to see enough to avoid embarrassing myself. I was the only one in the auditorium who didn't have a clear picture of what was happening. I wondered, is the first man the principal or the superintendent? Whose hand do I shake, and who is going to hand me my diploma? As usual, I pulled it off without divulging my sight impairment. As usual, that was the most important thing to me.

In many ways this walk symbolized my whole life up to that point as well as my life moving forward. The diploma I clutched was like a grand trophy presented to me at the conclusion of my four-year struggle to dream. But, I had only begun to struggle, and I had only begun to dream.

CHAPTER 5

SUMMER OF '64

During the summer that followed graduation from high school, I worked with my father every day. There had always been something special about working with him, more so now than ever. I could play an important role by doing whatever was the most physically demanding—and there was always plenty that was physically demanding. My father took advantage of the fact that I had developed the build of a football player, and I could also work like one.

While not necessarily intellectually stimulating, the work gave me a sense of satisfaction because I could contribute in a meaningful way. When your father is in the plumbing and water well repair business, digging ditches is routine. By the summer of 1964, I told everyone I had earned a Ph.D. in ditch digging: "pile higher and deeper."

I could pretty well count on digging ditches at least one day per week, usually the hottest. I remember one afternoon when my father and I went to install a water system for a couple who lived outside of town. The goal was to install a pump and filtration system in the well house at the top of the hill and to run a pipeline down the hill into the earthen pond below. As usual, it was my job to dig the ditch.

That summer was the hottest ever recorded. I don't know whether there was any Biblical significance to it or not, but for 40 days and 40 nights the daytime high never once failed to reach 100 degrees. When my brother and I drove through town at midnight one night, the temperature on the bank thermometer stood at an even 100 degrees.

My father fully expected that I would be right alongside him in all aspects of the business and he enjoyed telling people that I was his "little" boy. His little boy hauled pea gravel, 400 pounds at a time, pulled pipe from water wells, and swung a sledgehammer—all while the thermometer registered in the triple digits, day after day.

While we also did a whole host of lighter plumbing repairs ranging from fixing faucets, toilets, and air conditioners to cleaning out clogged drains, the more physically demanding the job, the more I enjoyed it. These tasks did not require good eyesight—just the ability to keep both eyes open and remain alert. Even with my poor eyesight, I could manage that. The fact that I could excel at these chores is what drove me. Working hard, whether at school or on the job, had always been deeply satisfying. Work for me would always be its own best reward because of the challenge it presented. Then as now, achieving results is the antithesis of being disabled. Having an opportunity to earn my father's approval made it all the sweeter.

The opportunity to be really good at something was quite empowering and freeing, so there was never any question in my mind that I would succeed at whatever task I was assigned. No one who saw me doing such heavy work ever suspected that I was legally blind. It was the opposite reaction I received when people saw me struggling two or three inches from my schoolwork—those people couldn't imagine me in any role that was independent. To them, I was a poor unfortunate soul to be pitied.

Earning a paycheck every two weeks was also satisfying, even though I didn't have a car or any social life to speak of to spend the money on. Getting paid for the hard, backbreaking work I did reinforced my sense of self-worth.

All too often, people with impairments miss out on the satisfaction that comes from being fulfilled through work. Such individuals, more than most, need someone to provide at least the psychological equivalent of a paycheck.

That someone for me was my father. The more I matured, the richer my relationship with him became. He was a phenomenal source of intellectual growth and inspiration for a boy who had largely been excluded from traditional sources of mental stimulation. The more I developed, the more I felt a sense of divine providence that God had provided me a personal tutor of the very highest order.

My father had been forced to quit school after the eighth grade to support his mother and younger half-brother when his mother divorced for the second time.

Even so, he got accepted at the largest pharmacy school in the United States at the time, located in Macon, Georgia, even though he never attended high school. At age 17, he graduated number one in his class. During World War II, when my father was stationed at Fort Sill, Oklahoma, he served as one of two instructors in the Officers Candidate School. What made this so remarkable was the fact that he was elevated from the rank of Private Third Class to officer status and made an instructor shortly after arriving at the fort. Out of 2,000 recruits given an intelligence exam, he received the highest score.

This created a dilemma for some of the top brass, who instead quickly selected the captain who earned the second highest score—they did not want to promote a private to this position. Nonetheless, my father was eventually selected. This was neither the first nor last time that someone in authority attempted to deny him what he had rightfully earned. After graduating from pharmacy school, Dad returned to Texas and traveled to Austin to apply for his license. The person authorized to issue the license realized my father was very young and asked his age, while reminding him that a person had to be 21 years old in Texas to receive such a license. Rather than lie about his age, he left empty-handed, leaving a promising career behind forever. After working at Mineral Wells Pipe & Supply with his uncle and aunt for several years, he decided to study to become a master plumber, by reading books on his own. In those days, master plumber exams were administered in one's hometown by someone already practicing in the community. Unfortunately, this arrangement provided the perfect opportunity for established plumbers to eliminate competition by simply failing applicants. When that happened to my father, he went to Austin to take the exam. Not surprisingly, he made the second highest score ever recorded on the exam in Texas. Dad never mentioned the name of the pharmacy school he had attended or the name of the plumber in Mineral Wells who tried to thwart his career—my mother shared all of this with me. It meant a lot to me that my father had encountered and overcome some major obstacles of his own. In this regard, as in so many other respects, he was a phenomenal mentor.

These achievements were an inspiration to me, especially given the fact that he was raised by an inattentive mother and absentee father. By the time I found out what he had gone through, I was nearly grown and had already lived in awe of my father for many years. I recognized it the way that one recognizes great music: inescapable and moving. While I was quiet in school and church, as well as around Janie, I talked incessantly to my father, in an effort to get my father to talk to me. From my earliest memory, he would spend virtually every available minute tending to Janie's considerable needs during the time he spent at home. And he spent every possible minute at home when he was not working. It was when I started working with him that I really appreciated him. This made the summer of 1964 very special.

. . .

When work was finished, that sense of being alone which had tormented me in high school always returned. Fortunately, my brother was home from college for the summer, and he and I would hang out with his friend, Ken Gruben.

Like my brother, Ken was extremely bright and witty. I enjoyed their company and the temporary relief from my sense of isolation. I wasn't always included, and that stung—in retrospect, I'm glad there were those times when my brother had some freedom from his kid brother.

Sometimes we would hunt birds. This worked out well because I could see the birds in flight against the contrasting sky. Sometimes we would hunt other animals, and I eventually became a decent shot. Anything I could do to feel independent and accomplished meant something to me. When shooting, I could hold my own—and my confidence soared.

In mid-July, I learned that my old childhood friend, Joe Moore, although a grade behind me, now had a steady girl and I knew he had been driving since the day he turned 16. I asked Joe if I might double-date with him and explained my desire to ask Barbara to go to the show. That's when Joe said, "She's going steady with a friend of mine." I had feared such a thing but was nonetheless disappointed.

Fortunately, the very next week, several of mother's brothers and sisters and their families came to Texas to visit. My grandfather had died the previous year. Granny, now completely alone, continued to live in the remote little farmhouse, a few miles from Post Oak, about an hour from Mineral Wells. Everyone had planned to get together at Granny's. Four of Granny's children, all adults, plus nine of us grandkids managed to gather there.

My cousin Terry and I hit it off right away, and I ended up spending a week with him at Granny's house. While I had turned 18 earlier that year, Terry was still 17 and not yet eligible to drive in his home state of Washington. Like most boys at that age, we were as interested in girls as we were cars, and I felt at liberty to pursue whomever I liked—although it was a liberty I had not wanted. Unfortunately, neither of us had a driver's license. He was too young and I was too blind. We were able to convince Uncle Bob, Terry's father, to let Terry drive the family car.

With the car problem solved, we did manage to hook up with Judy and Sandy. I had known Judy since we were small children. The four of us played basketball in the old sheet metal gymnasium which also served as the community center. To beat the heat, we went swimming in the spring-fed earthen tank which Judy's dad had built. About that time, it became apparent that Judy and Terry were developing feelings for each other and wanted to be alone. I never felt the same about Sandy—we remained "just friends." At the end of that week, it was time for Terry to return to Washington, so he and Judy said goodbye. Terry's family wanted to visit my mother for a few days, so we went to Mineral Wells.

The following Monday morning, Terry's family drove me back to Post Oak and let me out about two miles down the road from Granny's house. The adults reasoned that my going back for a week would ease Granny back into complete solitude. By crossing a couple of pastures, I only had to walk about a mile. This was good because I was carrying a suitcase in one hand and my .22 rifle (complete with scope) in the other.

As Terry and his family drove away, I sat down my suitcase and proceeded to wave enthusiastically, imagining they were doing the same. Then I struggled to get myself, my luggage, and my firearm over the barbed-wire fence which paralleled the dirt road—and which I had a challenge to see clearly.

Though nearly a half a century has lapsed since that July morning, I remember how the blue sky was polka-dotted with small white clouds as I began to make my way around the various obstacles in the pasture. I was forced to keep my eyes focused on the terrain immediately in front of me. There were endless clumps of needle grass, which contained hundreds of tiny little barbs, each eager to cling to your socks and pant legs. There were almost as many patches of prickly pears to be avoided. I had to pick a path that would be clear of stumps and small mesquite trees which were draped with thorns—no easy task for someone legally blind. Add to that the possibility of snakes, although it was fairly uncommon to encounter one. I did have my trusty weapon, and knew how to shoot it if I had to. Like the early settlers, I kept a firearm on my person and wore leather boots to protect against snakes.

In many ways, this walk was an analogy of my life: I couldn't begin to see my destination and had to struggle to see how to take the next step—still, I had a sense of direction and a sense of confidence. What is more, it was like going home, since I had visited that old farm and neighboring pastures a hundred times or more and had nothing but good memories of being there. Some of those memories were of Judy, whom I had known since we were 6 or 7 years old. The most recent of those memories were but a few days old, when my proximity to her had revealed her transition from tomboy to attractive young woman with a personality to match. I was hoping the week ahead would bring us together now that my cousin was out of the picture. However, for that to happen, a major barrier would have to be removed. She had chosen Terry, and my interest in being someone's second choice was somewhere between zero and not at all. As I saw it, Judy needed to make the first move.

It was good to see Granny again, and as always she seemed glad to see me. It was about 11 o'clock, and I began to put away my things while Granny started lunch. She seemed pleased to have someone else for whom to cook.

On that first afternoon back at Granny's, I ran into Judy's younger brother, Donald, as I was walking. Even though Donald was only 12, he was driving his dad's wreck of a 1956 Ford pickup. He invited me to get in and go with him in search of "big game."

Donald shared my interest in the outdoors. We went hunting or fishing nearly every day that week. He didn't care that I couldn't see well, and I didn't care that he was only 12. Because I was hanging around with Donald, I knew Judy would know I was there. Each evening, I hoped she would show up in her family's new Mercury that became available to her once her mom got home from work.

Finally, on Saturday night, after my parents had arrived to get me and to visit Granny, Judy and Donald showed up. They asked if I wanted to go to their house for a while. Since I had a couple of hours to kill before we headed back to Mineral Wells, I jumped in and off we went. Almost immediately, it was obvious that Judy wanted to get me alone. While this would have thrilled me even one day earlier, I was now just frustrated. I felt like I was a second choice—after all, she had chosen Terry last week. Even at such a young and immature age, I approached my relationships seriously. I couldn't help but think that her initial preference for Terry was influenced by my disability. In the end, I was determined to make something of myself and thus deserved to be someone's first choice. I was not about to settle for less.

CHAPTER 6

SMALL LEAPS

As summer drew to a close, I began making arrangements to attend Weatherford Junior College—the more respectable term of community college had not yet come into common use. The plan was for me to live at home and attend school part-time. Situated in its namesake community 20 miles east of Mineral Wells, the campus was the closest college to home. The school's proximity was crucial to me, since I would have to find someone to ride with. By commuting with Ken, who had become a good friend to me while remaining Jimmy's best buddy, I was able to attend class three days a week.

This schedule accommodated my work schedule—I was able to continue working for my father 15–20 hours per week, and earn money for school expenses, including supplies, snacks, and lunches, reducing my parents' financial outlays to tuition of $50 (about $300 in 2016 dollars). My father and Uncle John benefited from this arrangement, as it provided them an able-bodied helper. Having someone available who knew what they were doing and wasn't afraid to work hard was as good for them as for me. But believe me—I earned every cent I was paid.

For the four years leading up to my starting college, my parents had paid all of Jimmy's expenses to attend school away from home. Jimmy worked every summer at our local Piggly Wiggly so he could buy and maintain his own car. By the time he left for Texas Tech, he was on his third set of wheels, a sharp-looking 6-year-old Chevy. However, he blew an engine, which meant my parents needed to come to his rescue. My living at home while commuting to school would help save my parents the expense of room and board.

My first view of the school's campus was when Ken parked his dad's car about 200 feet down the street from the main campus, in front of the school's old wooden gymnasium. If this structure was any indication of what the rest of the campus was like, I thought we were in trouble. But, a few steps closer changed everything: we were standing in front of the institution's crown jewel. The Academic Building was constructed of large sandstone blocks more than two feet thick, reminding me of the Alamo. Once inside, I was struck by the tall ceilings and antique decor.

After we made our way to the registration area, Ken helped me examine the courses available at the times we would both be on campus. I selected English, History, Math, and a required one-hour course, Freshman Orientation.

A few weeks after the semester began, I dropped out of Math. Not being able to see what the instructor was writing on the board, combined with not being able to see the book well enough to read the instructions and examples, proved overwhelming.

English was interesting but challenging because it was focused on grammar and writing, with very little literature. Despite my limitations, I loved writing because it allowed me to be creative. Grammar was a challenge because I couldn't focus on it the way I could with writing.

The course consisted primarily of writing compositions in class. Mrs. Bailey, our instructor, would mark up the errors and return the essays. Needless to say, I had a great deal of difficulty reading her corrections but there was an even bigger problem: many of the errors were spelling mistakes. The list of English words which can be misspelled is even more exhaustive than the rules of grammar.

Although I had never been able to sit down and study books on grammar, over the years I have heard most of the rules stated aloud. This was not the same as having read properly punctuated materials since early childhood, as evidenced by my poor grades when it came to grammar. Learning to spell was even worse. In grade school, we were given a list of words to memorize each week. This was something that my mother could help me with while cooking meals; I learned these lists in a flash, given that my lack of vision forced me to fine-tune other skills, including listening and memorization. Such drills generally involved 25 words per week and lasted through the eighth grade. However, this proved a poor substitute for having read tens of thousands of words tens of thousands of times during the first 18 years of life, as my peers had done. It seemed such an irony that the only subject in which I had consistently excelled during elementary and junior high would prove my greatest area of weakness in college.

I realized that there was no way of knowing how to spell English words without memorizing them. I knew that many sounds were spelled one way in one word and another very different way in another word. Here's what I mean: the word "regard" has no "u" even though the word "guard" does.

I have since learned that there are 240 spellings for the 40 sounds in English. Thus, there are, on average, six ways to spell every sound. This means you need to memorize to spell, which in turn means you need to see or feel each letter. I could do neither.

Most people couldn't figure me out, and didn't understand why my spelling was so poor. It was frustrating to me that teacher after teacher assumed that because I didn't spell well, I was not intelligent. They focused on how I spelled, instead of the content of what I wrote. Even my parents concluded that my inability to learn to spell merely reflected an inability to sound out words. They laughed about it but did nothing to help, as they assumed that it was just "the way I was."

I wonder if it would have helped had I produced expert testimony explaining that there are, as I mentioned above, an average of six ways to spell each sound in English. I doubt that such information would have changed many perceptions.

The damage that poor spelling would exact upon my grade in freshman English was a harbinger of things to come. To Mrs. Bailey's credit, she did not dismiss me intellectually because of my awful spelling, marginal handwriting, and mediocre grammar. Other instructors were not as forgiving or encouraging—instead, they chose to write me off.

Fortunately for me, Mrs. Bailey made it a practice to give two grades on essays written in class. One measured content; the other measured grammar and spelling. Actually, I was never sure whether this was a classwide practice or one she used just for me. Regardless, I typically received an A/D: an A for content and a D for grammar and spelling. The bad news was that the A was cosmetic, and the D went into the gradebook. Because Mrs. Bailey was there to teach us spelling and grammar, my literary potential went unnoticed grade-wise. I quickly reached the conclusion that your grade in freshman English was more a function of the grammar and spelling skills you possessed when entering the room on the first day than on your efforts during the semester. However, I am most grateful to Mrs. Bailey for acknowledging my skills when it came to content.

She brought me copies of writers' magazines that, admittedly, I could not see, except for the boldest print and the pictures. Nonetheless, those magazines sent a message to me that she cared: where other instructors had dismissed me because I couldn't see, Mrs. Bailey saw potential.

...

Dean Daniels, whom I had known at Mineral Wells High, and was also in Mrs. Bailey's class, invited me to go with him to the Baptist Student Union (BSU) one morning when we both had some free time. I went once and never stopped going. Being involved with the BSU meant being around other students who shared my faith, without being in a strict traditional church environment. It became my "third place"—my home away from home. I felt like I had always belonged there. The relationships that I developed there had a life-changing impact on how I approached my life going forward. I knew that my life was in the hands of the Lord, and that He would see me through any challenge I would face from that point on.

Mr. Cody, my American History instructor, had a great combination of energy and sense of humor. He was tough but fair, and like Mrs. Bailey, saw my potential. He met with me in private to administer each test. Sometimes he gave me the test personally, and sometimes he arranged for a student grader to administer it. I became nervous when he administered the test himself. Although he volunteered to do this and never acted the least bit imposed upon, I was not accustomed to causing such inconvenience to adults.

Mr. Cody's classes consisted of lectures broken only by his dreaded pop quizzes and his even more dreaded exams. Unlike English class, the majority of what we would be graded on in history was information we learned in class. The upside to this was that by listening and taking thorough notes, I could get by without reading the textbook.

Taking notes was a challenge. Slumped over a desk in my typical less-than-debonair posture, I wrote fast, half seeing and half drawing from memory the letters I formed in my mind. Once I got home, I would rewrite my notes very slowly with a bold, black pen.

My high-speed penmanship was even worse than my already awful "regular" writing. However, my well-developed memory and an occasional burst of legibility helped me to transform the messy pages into discernible English words.

However, this painful process helped me in two ways. The review reinforced what I had learned in class, and the product which resulted enabled me to read my notes long after the lectures were over. I persisted, despite the task of reading the notes pertaining to a single test generally requiring a couple of hours or more of effort. Whether such a task was too demanding was never a question. If I could do it, I did it. Unlike my peers, I didn't have a choice. When the semester was over, my considerable efforts produced a C in history—for me, the equivalent of having gotten nominated to the honor roll. I was thrilled. I had beaten the odds and the naysayers who thought I couldn't do it.

Freshman Orientation class was taught by Mr. Locke, who also taught a course or two in psychology and served as the college's official counselor. Mr. Locke represented the brick walls I would face in school and beyond.

However, just then, he was teaching us about how to succeed as a college student. His stories and examples were fascinating, and I took notes and absorbed everything he was telling us. Unfortunately, the course required reading, and as usual, I struggled. I also struggled with his exams—they were not only long, they were "objective." Unlike essay tests, where I could read one or two sentences and then write a lengthy answer, these exams forced me to read long questions and provide short answers. My vision made this a next-to-impossible undertaking, and getting through a question one time was a major accomplishment. Re-reading for clarity and as a means of double-checking was out of the question. I was sunk.

Unlike Mr. Cody, Mr. Locke never offered to give me my exams in private, or to accommodate me in any way. In fact, to me it seemed as if he was trying to do anything possible to see me fail. After awarding me a D in the course, he told me that I needed to learn to ask others for help. While at the time I hated his advice, I now realize he was correct in his assessment—I didn't feel the least bit inclined to ask anyone to do anything for me. The focus of my childhood had been to look for ways to help my parents and Janie, and not on asking for help myself. It just never dawned on me that it was not only acceptable to ask for help, it was essential.

...

Right before I started school that fall, a case worker from the Texas Commission for the Blind informed me that I really didn't have much of a chance of succeeding in college, as I hadn't even graduated in the top half of my high school class. I suppose if I had placed in the 49th percentile instead of the 53rd, he would have anticipated smooth sailing for me. The very fact that he knew I had been denied all the services of his agency throughout high school— and still managed to do better than half of my *sighted* classmates—made his remarks even more ludicrous. To me, he was admitting that his agency's services didn't work and weren't valuable.

I had seen enough of these self-styled authority figures who presumed to be more intelligent than I was, simply because I had trouble seeing. While he felt he was instructing me about the cold, hard realities that would face me going forward, I chose to look beyond his dire prediction, and instead focused on the positive influencers—and influences—in my life. There had been others before, and there would be more in the future. For whatever reason, some people resented my ambition and audacious goals and felt obliged to help me face the truth that I would never amount to anything.

Even so, I managed to take advantage of some of the services the agency offered. One of these was a Talking Book Machine.

A Talking Book Machine was essentially a record player. In fact, you could use it to play phonograph records. Its real value, however, was its ability to play small limber plastic discs containing spoken material. These machines were furnished free of charge to legally blind people for many years, courtesy of the National Library of Congress. In the mid-1960s, this was state of the art technology.

During my first semester, I didn't have any of my books on record. I was still in denial about being "legally blind" and didn't want to accept the facts of my circumstances. The case worker's attitude towards me didn't help.

When the semester was over, even though my grades were disappointing, I had made it through my first semester of college. Not the least bit dissuaded, I looked to a much more ambitious second semester. I was energized by having made it on my own through the first semester. Having found a way to get to the campus five days a week, I enrolled in 15 hours of coursework. I felt that the amount of time available for each course would have far less impact on my grades than the instructional format used in each course.

I reasoned that lecture courses would require less reading than those requiring either considerable textbook work or a heavy reliance on a chalk-board. Although I knew that the second half of freshman English was going to be tough, I didn't have a choice. Besides, it was once again taught by Mrs. Bailey so I knew I at least had a chance, although I didn't feel I could ever earn a decent grade. Nonetheless, I knew that taking a small class load wouldn't help and didn't want to be a student for the rest of my life.

Dean McClung, the dean of admissions, made note of the full course load in light of the fact that I had not taken the Scholastic Aptitude Test (SAT). He contacted Mr. Locke, my former Freshman Orientation instructor, and asked him to give me an intelligence test.

Mr. Locke announced that he was going to give me a portion of an I.Q. test. After the test was completed, I had a feeling that I had done very well—in fact, extremely well. However, Mr. Locke offered no information once I finished, so I pressed him for information a few days later. He informed me that I had performed "a little above average." I didn't believe this was accurate. This wasn't hubris on my part—instead it was my own experience and confidence. For the time being I would just go on believing better things about my abilities and doing my best with limited tools.

. . .

During that second semester, Ms. Smith, head of the History Department, was one of my instructors. On my first day in her class I realized that I had been all wrong about Mr. Cody in American History. He hadn't talked fast at all. Ms. Smith left him in the dust.

As demanding as Ms. Smith was, her course was limited to lecture materials—perfect for me. I received an A- on the objective portion and a B+ on the essay portion of her first major exam. I was elated. This was one of the highest grades in a large class.

None of my other courses that semester were well suited to my visual challenges, primarily because I had none of my textbooks on record. I barely passed my other classes, but I made a high B in history.

Finally, during my third semester, I managed to acquire one textbook on record, my literature book for sophomore English. It was pretty ironic that my first talking book concerned itself with Greek Mythology. I found it hard to be interested in the material, but I forced myself. While my writing was still a disaster, I managed to score well enough on the literature element to get a C in the course. I managed to squeak by in my other courses, despite the fact I wasn't able to read the textbooks for my classes.

Finally, I reached par for an entire semester by earning a C average. I had taken less than a full academic load, which allowed me to be called up for the Vietnam War that, by 1965, was escalating. I was ready and willing to go because I thought there were plenty of jobs that I could do well, even with my poor eyesight. If the draft board saw it that way, I was ready to fulfill my obligation to my country. If not, the issue would be settled once and for all. Needless to say, I received a permanent 4F. I actually had mixed emotions about not being drafted—I wanted to feel that I was "normal" like everyone else being drafted. But I was enormously relieved that I would never have to worry about fighting strangers in a strange land.

As we headed back toward Mineral Wells that day, I observed the other young men and a wave of sadness washed over me. These boys were mostly poor and, frankly, not very intelligent from what I could observe. It was pretty obvious why many of them weren't able to receive a college deferment. Life had already been unkind to most of these young men. I wondered why our country was singling them out for the dirtiest of our dirty work, but I already knew the answer.

Since the bus went right through Weatherford on the way home and I still had an hour or so before my regular ride would be leaving campus, I got off the bus at the square downtown. This allowed me to check on some of my assignments before going home. As I walked the mile or so to campus, I continued to feel melancholy about the boys who were being sent to Vietnam—many of whom would not return alive—and sorry for myself that I would never even have the option.

...

By the fourth semester, I was in a better position to get all my books on record. As I began to make plans, I confided in the director of the BSU, James Heath, whom had become a friend and confidante.

Jim was a doctoral candidate at Southwestern Theological Seminary in nearby Fort Worth. Brilliant and fun-loving, he left you with the impression that he was quiet and unassertive. After a year of knowing him, I would learn that nothing could be further from the truth.

Jim told me that I needed $8 a week for rent. While not a lot of money back then, it was still a stretch. Reluctantly, I broached the subject with my father, knowing that times were not good, and Jimmy had already been away at college for four years when I started. I could tell Dad was reluctant but he finally consented—I'm sure he realized how important it was for me to be independent.

In January of 1966, my parents took me to my new home. Once I got unpacked, there was just enough time for me to make my way to church. Rev. Williams, the seminary student/pastor of the Emmanuel Baptist Church, had met me at the BSU and asked me to attend his church when I got to town.

I had just about completed the two-mile walk out of town to the church in 32-degree and snowy weather when Rev. Williams and his wife stopped to offer me a lift. Though I couldn't see them at all, I recognized their car, a 1964 Oldsmobile. I jumped in.

Immediately, just as I had at the BSU, I felt at home in this church. After the service, I was urged to stay for a youth fellowship. It was there I met the church pianist, who, at 17, was very different than I had imagined before seeing her up close. My chance meeting of this young woman proved an omen of good things to come. I learned her name was Carolyn, and didn't expect to encounter her again outside of church—but I was wrong. Only a couple of days later, as I was about to enter a restaurant for lunch, I heard someone call my name. It was Carolyn, and the restaurant I was entering belonged to her parents.

...

As the semester got underway, I was thrilled at having all my books on record. The semester which followed was much more gratifying than the previous three had been.

After three semesters of hit or miss schedules that had added up to roughly two good semesters worth of courses and less than a C average, for the first time in my life, I had a way to read, with reasonable speed, all of my books.

Immediately, I began to make very solid Bs. In fact, I was consistently within striking distance of an A in every course. My academic dreams had come true. I was among the top four or five students in every class. For someone who had been told he would never amount to much, I was finally on my way.

During that semester, Carolyn and I began dating. An unusually mature high school senior, she was also extraordinarily bright, attractive, levelheaded, and a good soul. In other words, not your typical teenager. Ours was the type of first significant relationship that every person should have.

Because I ate both lunch and supper at her family's restaurant, she and I would eat together every night. Our talks were open and stimulating, and we discussed everything except my limited vision and the tools I required to cope with it, and her brilliant academic standing. After years of conditioning to minimize and even hide my disability, I never said that I used a talking book machine or that I couldn't read normal print. She never said she would be graduating third in a class of 197.

When my final grades were posted, I was disappointed twice. A perfect storm of circumstances had conspired that made it possible for the A I'd hoped for in government to deteriorate to a C. My instructor had decided to make the final exam count as much as all the other exams combined and to make it comprehensive. This meant that it would cover the entire book rather than just one section as each of the other tests had done.

This proved especially challenging for me, since I was limited to the use of a talking book machine. Unlike the other students, I could not scan the book to refresh my memory, and time would not permit me to reread the entire book. Thus, I had to rely entirely on what I could remember. Had I been told earlier in the semester that the final would be comprehensive, I could have saved each test and prepared large handprinted notes of highlights.

I received a grade of 79 in the course, and no allowance was made for the fact that I had been forced to use a substitute textbook. No one took into consideration that I had been at the top of the class in this course—a course that had a reputation for being a killer. I felt like all of my hard work had been wiped out in an instant. The irony was that my instructor had volunteered at the outset of the course to give me an extra point or two at the end of the semester if needed to reach the next letter grade. Obviously, she forgot her promise by semester's end.

I had never imagined any set of circumstances that could cause my grade to drop below a B. Suddenly, my goal of going from borderline student to one on the honor roll was destroyed.

What happened to me in psychology was even worse. Mr. Locke, the brick wall I mentioned earlier, took what I considered to be an obviously self-serving approach to grading. He simply refused to tell anyone his grade on any test throughout the semester. The highest possible score on one of Mr. Locke's exams was the same as the number of questions. For example, our first exam contained 61 questions, and I got 54 questions correct, meaning I had earned a 54.

There were only one or two higher scores in the large class. When I inquired whether this would be an A or a B, he merely replied, "Your grade is 54."

Mr. Locke had often spoken openly in class about his intention to produce a grade distribution that would provide a perfect bell curve. He even went so far as to admit that this would make him look good. I had gotten the feeling early on that Mr. Locke had no intention of allowing me to score higher on his bell curve than the place he envisioned for me at the outset. What is more, a grade of 79 was a little above average—in keeping with his assessment of my I.Q. Curiously, that semester, he offered to administer each of my exams in person, one-on-one. I actually looked forward to his exams because I spent more time preparing for his course than for the other three courses I was taking. Routinely, I answered at least 85% of the questions correctly. For that reason, I had been surprised to receive a C in his course at mid-semester, while the other three grades were Bs.

When I went to see him to check on my final grade, he told me I had earned "about a 79."

It had become clear during the semester that Mr. Locke had it out for me; honestly, I'm not sure why. He made it a practice to call me "Eight-ball Ashby," thinking it was amusing. Instead, it was demoralizing. We've all dealt with mean people in our lives, and I'm sure each of us can recall a teacher or instructor who should have been doing anything but teaching. Mr. Locke was one of those people; at least in his treatment of me. The irony is that he was clearly academically brilliant and a very interesting professor. I feel sure that many students over the years thought he was great.

During my lifetime, I have never known anyone who lent so much credence to the saying that psychology is "the study of the id by the odd." Mr. Locke, in my estimation, fit the typology of a person who was only comfortable allowing an individual with a disability to achieve at a level he felt appropriate, but nothing more. Some people suffer from a type of insecurity that causes them to erect a "glass ceiling" that inflicts pain on others because of it.

My first ever experience with having a textbook I could actually read in every course should have resulted in my name appearing on the B honor roll. In retrospect, I was probably too forthcoming with Carolyn, telling her about the two Bs and two Cs. I should probably have disclosed that semester as having been my first to have books to read—the outcome would not have been as shocking to her as it no doubt was. Because she made the initial move to promote the relationship, and we had enjoyed so many great conversations, I felt more confident than I should have. I thought she realized that I was as brilliant as she and that that conviction could withstand the temporary setback of my grades. Such was the kind of faith I was looking for. Rather quickly, it became apparent Carolyn was not prepared to place such faith in me, and for perfectly good reasons. Regardless of her assessment of my mental ability and determination to succeed in life, the timing was simply wrong. She did not need to enter college encumbered with a steady guy, and we were almost certainly headed for different schools. During our last real discussion, she spoke of how she had changed, and how her sister and brother-in-law—who had recently graduated from Rice University—had just bought a huge automobile. In retrospect, it was significant to me that she had never spoken of her plans to attend any specific university or volunteered any information about scholarships she had been offered, and given her class ranking, she almost certainly received several.

While I was disappointed about the parting of ways, I mainly felt a sense of gratitude for the many hours of joy we had shared—most of which were spent in simple conversation. There was no doubt in my mind that the girl I would settle down with would be equally delightful and interesting to talk with. Looking back, her failure to talk about her college aspirations and opportunities was entirely in keeping with her practice of being modest almost to a fault. Perhaps she was headed to Rice or some other Ivy League school and didn't want to lord it over me. All I do know is that she aspired to become a classroom teacher. Perhaps her older sister, whom I never met, warned her about becoming entangled with someone like me—someone with a major disability. Whatever factors influenced Carolyn to make the decision she did, I never detected a single personality flaw in Carolyn, and choose to remember her that way. The truth is, we never talked about getting serious, although, as the semester drew to a close, I did let her know she was special. And so she was. Knowing Carolyn made me realize I would never be content with a girl who was not a great conversationalist, and I never was.

CHAPTER 7

INSULT TO INJURY

When Dad and I knocked off work on a Friday in August of 1966, it was 110 degrees. We got cleaned up and made our first 40-mile trip to Stephenville, home to Tarleton State College. I had planned to attend Texas Tech University in Lubbock until my sister-in-law, a student at Tech, told me there was no housing available. Because this piece of intelligence came at the 11th hour, I found myself confronted with several hurdles, the most immediate of which was gaining admission, so my father and I headed straight to the office of the dean of admissions.

My father began to explain why I was seeking admission so late, and I explained my interest in majoring in history and government. I also explained my visual limitations and past academic performance. The dean asked Dr. Grant, the number two person in the Department of Social Sciences, to meet with us personally because both history and government were under his purview. Dr. Grant lived several blocks away, and walked to the campus in triple-digit temperatures just to meet with us. It seemed like we were off to a good start.

The next hurdle was finding a place to live. By this time the dorms were full, but we did manage to find a rooming house located about a half mile from the campus. Given that I couldn't drive, this wasn't a great solution but it could have been worse—besides, I didn't really have a choice.

On the way home that same day, I began to feel sick, and my temperature started to climb. Within an hour or so, it reached 105 degrees. My mother began trying to reach the family doctor while pumping aspirin down me. Finally, about midnight, the fever broke, and I was sleeping soundly by the time the doctor returned Mama's call early the following morning.

The next day we went to the doctor's office—it turned out I had a serious infection from an ingrown toenail. It required surgery, but I would have to wait six weeks before I could have the procedure. While the infection healed enough to have the surgery, I would be forced to walk on the affected foot— and suffer. This was bad enough for someone who had to walk from his house to the car, but the half mile I had to walk to school proved to be a killer.

After the six weeks passed and the infection had subsided, it made more sense for me to have the surgery locally instead of returning to Mineral Wells. The doctor who ended up performing the procedure proceeded to remove my big toenail with a pair of surgical pliers—without having properly applied local anesthetic!

This experience became symbolic of the mental pain I would experience throughout that first year. During that entire year, I had the ever-present feeling of not being in control. This was in painful contrast to my final semester at Weatherford. Because I had all of my textbooks on record during that last semester, I finally felt completely confident.

Despite feeling welcome by the dean, arriving on campus at the last possible minute meant that I didn't know the names of the textbooks I would need ahead of time. For most students, this wasn't a big deal, of course—they simply picked up their books at the school's bookstore right before classes began. But for me, it meant a delay of several weeks in receiving books on record, putting me behind before I even got started. A second, more serious problem emerged: as a junior, I was taking almost all advanced courses, and quickly found out that textbooks for advanced courses were far more difficult to acquire on short notice.

While I could request that new books be recorded, this process would take most or all of the semester. What all of this meant was that I had only one textbook available on record—I had to go through Algebra, Advanced Political Science, Advanced History, and French without any way to read the material that was a part of the coursework. To exacerbate my situation, in Algebra, classes centered around material written on the chalkboard—information I had no chance of seeing, and therefore, no chance of recording manually. I thought I could glean whatever I needed from the class lectures but realized too late that I also needed the required books.

The semester was agonizing. Because I couldn't access the books, I couldn't study the way I was used to studying. I hated feeling like I wasn't in control. I needed to perform a miracle, something I was used to doing. For me, miracles were born of necessity, not ego. At Weatherford College, it was a miracle that I had been able to elevate myself from a marginal student to one producing an average grade of 85; at Tarleton, it would be a miracle if I could survive the semester at all.

Recognizing my dilemma, I met with my counselor, Dr. Richard Smith, head of the Department of Government. He suggested that I adjust my schedule to drop certain problem courses such as Algebra. He also recommended cutting my course load to 12 semester hours. I thought I had found a kindred spirit in Dr. Smith—someone who could empathize with me. Finally, someone understood my abilities and limitations—someone who wanted to work with me, and help me succeed. I could not have been more mistaken.

At that time, Tarleton had a requirement that students must pass a minimum number of hours each semester, regardless of grade point average. I had fewer course hours, but that made my schedule absolutely unforgiving—I was required to pass 12 credit hours (four academic courses), which meant I had been set up for failure.

Dr. Smith himself failed me, despite the fact that I had passed every test in his course up to the final exam—and knowing my course load and visual challenges. Looking back on the experience, I believe Dr. Smith felt compelled to put me in my place: even though my spelling and writing was poor, I told him I hoped to one day write a textbook myself. Apparently, Dr. Smith felt that was too audacious a goal for someone like me. The very person responsible for my having been placed on the edge would be the one to push me off. One of the most humiliating and frustrating episodes of my life resulted: I was placed on scholastic probation.

To add insult to injury, Dr. Smith once again insisted that I take no more than four courses during my second semester at the school. I pleaded for permission to take additional courses, arguing that it wasn't fair to penalize me for being handicapped (like other forms of discrimination, bias against the disabled was common in the 1960s). All I could think of while I reasoned with him was that his decision could cause me to fail, and force me to drop out of school.

Dr. Smith seemed irritated that I would even question his judgment, and the answer was an emphatic *no*. It became clear that Dr. Smith didn't think I should be afforded a college education because of my disability—college was reserved for "normal" students. He once again set me up for failure.

I spent the entire semester knowing that even if I were to earn three As and one F, the results would be devastating, and my dream of earning a college degree would be over. If I failed anything, that would be it. Compounding my challenge, I was only able to secure two books on record.

The semester was full of uneasiness, frustration—and insults. One particularly cold and drizzly morning, I walked over to the infirmary to be treated for a sore throat instead of going to my 7:30 economics class. I was asked, in a voice loud enough so everyone around me could hear, if I was on scholastic probation. I was then told that I could not be excused from class to be treated because I was on probation. At that time, and at that school, you could not miss a class or receive a note from the infirmary if you were on scholastic probation. I was not only treated as an academic failure, I was refused medical treatment.

...

During this semester, I had a roommate—a first for me.

John Michael Davidson was not only brilliant, as a fellow BSU regular, he understood and embraced many of the same beliefs as I did. He encouraged me by always reminding me that I was smart. Like my other friends from the BSU, he saw past my disability and recognized my gifts.

BSU was the common thread among my friends during those years. At Tarleton, the BSU was a home away from home for Baptist students. Just as it had been at Weatherford, it was my "third place."

Almost all my friends were quintessential Texas farm boys, especially close friends Billy Brookshire and Glenn Blankenship. Their friendships would prove the most important that I would develop at Tarleton. They didn't judge me, patronize me, or pity me because I had a disability. Instead, they treated me like any other person—and helped me maintain my confidence during some pretty challenging years.

I taught Billy and Glenn how to play ping-pong. I had developed an aggressive style that compensated for my visual limitations. My technique was simple: if it moves, kill it. I concentrated on learning how to serve hard and slam the ball from any position. The three of us spent many hours attacking the game—and it proved to be a great outlet for my frustrations. The game helped me work off my anxiety and forget my stress for a while. It was their friendship in particular that helped me to cope with the academic challenges that persisted through the semester. It was the first time I realized how powerful true friends were.

Predictably, as the semester progressed, my course standings fell into two groups. I had solid grades in two subjects and just barely passing grades in the others. Still, somehow I managed to pass every test going into finals.

Billy and I were among the last students on campus to finish taking our final exams, and most everyone had already left. Once the last exam was turned in, we headed—as was our custom—for the BSU. As luck would have it, seven or eight of our friends, about an even mix of boys and girls, had also been among the last to finish. We were all ready to let off some steam.

One of the guys had a pickup truck, so we all piled in and proceeded to ride around all night. We saw parts of Erath County that may have been missed by the native Indians. All the while, my state of mind kept me from joining in the fun—the anxiety and mental pain of the semester had taken its toll, and I still didn't know whether I would be coming back for my senior year, or going home in disgrace.

When the next day finally came, we went around campus checking on how we had done in each course. I knew the moment of truth was at hand, and felt queasy.

Each time we came to another door where one of my grades was posted, my heart raced and I developed a huge lump in my throat. Although I felt almost certain that I would pass two of the courses with flying colors, I could not stop thinking about the fact that I had been denied the opportunity to take enough classes to guarantee that I would not get kicked out of school because of a single failure.

When we approached the door where our grades for the third course were posted, I could hear the unease in Billy's voice: "Walt, I'm afraid this one is bad." "How bad?" I asked reluctantly. "It's an F," he replied through a badly broken voice.

Right after that announcement, Billy's parents came for him, and I was suddenly alone—physically and figuratively.

The dorm was uncharacteristically quiet as I sat down on the concrete floor and leaned into the corner. For an hour or so I just sat there virtually motionless as though in a catatonic stupor.

All I could think about was that I couldn't even drive a delivery truck—just another college dropout with no prospects.

For me, a college degree was not a luxury; it was more than just the gateway to the grand horizons I had first imagined in Mrs. Downs's sophomore English class. It represented an opportunity for independence, achievement, and dignity.

At that moment, all hope of attaining these goals had been ripped from my hands—and my soul. There seemed to be absolutely no hope. There seemed to be only one way out—a final way—but this solution made no sense to me. It was contrary to everything I had believed in and stood for, yet not doing it seemed to lead nowhere. I had had a lifelong desire to bring to my parents an unexpected and wonderful outcome to my tragedy that might help ease their grief over Janie. Now it seemed that I might prove to be just another responsibility they didn't need.

While I thought about my options, I moved slowly across the narrow dormitory room to the drawer by the lavatory where I kept my shaving paraphernalia. The streams of tears which had saturated my cheeks turned to waterfalls as I removed my safety razor.

Ever so slowly, I turned and shuffled like a decrepit old man. Taking four or five small steps, I eventually reached the corner of the room where the outside door met the wall that ran alongside my bed. I sat down on the floor, leaned into that corner and absorbed one devastating emotional blow after another—each exploding upon impact like a miniature warhead delivered to its target.

Finally, after agonizing for more than an hour, I had an epiphany. I had an idea—a life-giving idea that brought hope. I would go see Dean Conyus, the dean of admissions, who had been so helpful to me when I first arrived at Tarleton. I figured at this point, I had nothing to lose but everything to gain. I put away the razor, and headed to the dean's office.

The dean was not only available; he wanted to help! I'm quite sure he could see the personal hell I was going through: my eyes were bloodshot from crying, and I didn't bother to even try to compose myself.

Dean Conyus informed me that the Academic Council would be meeting in a couple of weeks. He then assured me that he would discuss my situation with them and see if I could be permitted to return next fall. "If not," he reassured, "you will be allowed to return after skipping a semester." What I hadn't realized because I missed Freshman Orientation was that "flunking out" wasn't permanent—it was just a temporary setback. The Lord has sent me to Dean Conyus, and the dean saved me.

Finally, someone did understand—and tried to help me.

Later that day I left for the summer, still apprehensive but holding on to my newly found cause for hope.

CHAPTER 8

BLIND FAITH

Soon I would leave home and report for my summer job as the instructor at a rifle range. My mission was not to make marksmen out of the prepubescent monsters who were disguised as Boy Scouts, but to teach them the proper handling of firearms and some of the most basic techniques of shooting.

I had always loved guns and with the use of a scope had become quite skilled with a rifle—I had developed the skills required to point a shotgun with pretty good accuracy. I often felt I was living in two worlds: I was able to shoot well and even ride my motorbike, yet I struggled to read or write well.

When I arrived, the rifle range was a mess and virtually inaccessible because the trail leading to it had deteriorated so badly. I commandeered a wheelbarrow, pick, sledgehammer, and shovel and went to work, spending the next several days performing backbreaking labor—which proved to be extraordinarily therapeutic. Every swing of the pick or sledgehammer chipped away at my pent-up frustration. It was a relief to be able to get something done using my hands.

At the end of the first day, when I relaxed after supper, I realized what a great sense of mental and psychological relief I felt. I was sure I would be returning to Tarleton in the fall, and within a few days a letter from Dean Conyus' office confirmed that. This was a turning point in my life, and I never looked back: from that point on, I felt much more confident that I was going to go somewhere with my life.

. . .

Later on that summer I received another piece of good news: The State Commission for the Blind had increased the amount of money available for students to purchase reader service. The increase was substantial enough that I would be able to actually hire people to read my textbooks to me and also help me with special needs. As the fall semester got underway, the difference this made was amazing: I had much greater peace of mind, more self-assurance, and better grades on my early semester exams. After the mid-semester grades came out, I made a special trip by Dean Conyus' office to show him the results: five Bs and one C. With obvious pleasure in his voice, the distinguished, gray-haired dean said, "That's remarkable." I thought so as well.

As satisfying as these words were, this was the eighth year in a row that my parents had had a child in college, and my father's business had not been doing well for the past several years. Even so, my parents managed to scrape together the money to keep me in school.

Although they never said anything, I knew they were concerned that their investment in my education might be for naught. However, they kept at it, in great part to encourage me to be independent and to instill confidence in me.

My primary goal that semester was to make it onto the dean's honor roll. More specifically, I wanted to secure what was known as a "Blue Card." The traditional advantage of a Blue Card was that it allowed its owner (by definition, an honor student) to be excused from class, subject to certain restrictions, simply by displaying the card. Having a Blue Card gave you certain privileges, but more importantly let others know what you had achieved. It was more symbolic than anything, but it was a symbol I wanted to obtain.

Truth be told, I really had no desire to skip any classes—the card was a way for me to combat the discrimination I had experienced with many of my instructors. I accepted discrimination as a fact of life, but I wanted people to understand that having a physical disability doesn't mean you are a lesser person—you're just as smart (or stupid) as the next person. If I could display a Blue Card, it would effectively communicate to every instructor that I had a history of making either As or Bs. They would no longer assume that because I was visually impaired—legally blind, in fact—that I couldn't make it. Or worse, shouldn't expect to.

Unlike most Texas universities, Tarleton required a higher grade point average to make the dean's honor roll: 2.25 versus 2.0 at most other institutions. While I was below that level at mid-semester, I was within striking distance. I would have to pull up one B in a one-hour elective course to an A, and do the same in one three-hour academic course. I would also have to bring up that one C (which was in Dr. Smith's required course) or turn a third B into an A. With my newly-found confidence, this was entirely possible, since I held the highest B in the class in two or three different courses, and the C in Dr. Smith's course was a C+.

As the semester wore on, I focused on my strategy. During our Thanksgiving break, I took a friend home with me—a friend who also happened to be one of my best readers. This allowed me to get in some extra work on Dr. Smith's course. I returned to campus a week early during the Christmas break so I could complete an enormous term paper that I was sure would get me into A territory in another class.

During this same time, I began to date a freshman. Together, we went around campus to check on final grades. When she read aloud, in complete disbelief, the bad news that I had received an F in Dr. Smith's course, I had a completely different reaction than I had had the last semester. Instead of retreating into myself, I immediately went into his office and confronted him.

I was furious, and he was irritable and short with me. He pulled out my final exam and informed me that I had an F on the final and an F in the course.

I attempted to reason with him by stating that all I needed to pass the course was a 29 on the final. He handed me the exam and growled about how he could fail me in the course because I had failed the final. I responded by letting him know that I had a B average for the rest of my courses but would be discharged from school purely on this one F. He didn't care. In fact, he seemed to get a degree of satisfaction from failing me.

As this conversation was taking place, I managed to look through the exam enough to notice that Dr. Smith had only written two words on the second of the 13 pages: "VERY POOR." It was obvious that he hadn't bothered to read the rest of the exam.

At that moment I felt anger, frustration, distress, and, because my girl-friend was present, embarrassment. I stormed out of the room, but not before I grabbed the exam. This time, instead of heading to my dorm room, I headed straight for Dean Conyus' office.

As I explained what happened to the dean, and showed him the exam bearing an "F," I also showed him my major term paper for a different course—that paper had earned an "A." The contrast was absurd, as was the whole series of events. Even with the F in Dr. Smith's class, my grade point average was easily among the top 25%, yet here I was in the dean's office begging not to be discharged. I cannot explain how angry and disgusted I was knowing I had been discriminated against—and it was all perfectly legal.

Fortunately, I was able to separate the facts from my emotions. Dean Conyus agreed that I could have an opportunity to present my request for reinstatement directly to the Academic Council at the beginning of the spring semester in about three or four weeks.

Those weeks were anything but the break they were intended to be—instead, they were filled with constant anxiety. Even as I performed with the premier choir on campus during my break, my future at the school occupied my mind before, during, and after performances. The angst I was feeling was all-consuming.

When my day of reckoning arrived, I presented what I felt was a persuasive argument. I was escorted to a nearby room, where my girlfriend and I awaited their verdict.

To my relief, the Council agreed with me. I was exonerated. Not only did I receive permission to register for the spring semester, the Council completed its discussion and cast its favorable vote within a span of just 60 seconds. I was told I would never again be strapped with the additional handicap of a small course load. To have been discriminated against like that—and then winning the right to be treated like everyone else—was an amazing feeling. It was truly another life-altering event. While my girlfriend and I broke up soon after this, I learned that she had deliberately waited until the Counsel had reached its decision—she didn't want to leave me alone to face what might be devastating news.

I signed up for an extra course, and this time my schedule did not include any courses under Dr. Smith. I passed everything, again producing a very respectable grade point average. Finally, I got released from scholastic probation.

The emotional fatigue that had built up over the previous three semesters lingered as the fourth semester went on. For me, it was the psychological equivalent of asking an athlete who has just completed a three-hour race to run for an additional hour. I was emotionally exhausted.

. . .

The Tarleton Players, the theatrical group on campus, announced that it would be performing a musical in May and wanted to enlist the a cappella choir to which I belonged.

I approached the choir's director to see if there might be an acting role for me. The role of an old man in the chorus was perfect for me: I could stumble or otherwise appear half blind to my heart's content!

The old man stole the show, and I had a lot of fun in the process. While I failed to get an Oscar, I did capture the much-coveted "Rubber Ducky Award" bestowed at the cast party which followed closing night. My involvement in the play helped me cope with the stress I had been experiencing. I was finally officially removed from scholastic probation, freed from the trap Dr. Smith had set for me. I passed all 15 hours and, again, earned respectable grades. I now had a new goal: graduate school.

Dr. Smith was one of many who felt obliged to make me accept the unfortunate limitations which life had placed on me—by abandoning the goals toward which I aspired. Like many others, he was wrong.

Once the threat to my immediate academic well-being was finally and permanently conquered and I was able to select my own course load, my agenda shifted: I wanted to graduate as soon as possible and get into graduate school at a major university.

After consulting with some instructors in the school's psychology department, I found out that I was entitled to a complete psychological battery courtesy of the State Commission for the Blind. In fact, they recommended I insist on it.

I took their advice and contacted my counselor with the State Commission—the same man who, like Dr. Smith, seemed to want to pull me back instead of push me forward. He admitted that it was true that such a service was available but warned me that the only basis under which such a service would be provided would be for the use of my college counselors. They would have to get a copy of the results in writing. His inference was that the results would not be good. In other words, he was convinced that I was not very bright—presumably because I had not graduated in the top half of my high school class and had struggled at Weatherford and Tarleton when I had very few tools for acquiring the required study materials. He never got it that the other blind students he had known who had achieved consistent academic success had used Braille, Talking Book Machines, Reader Service, and a host of other services that I had never enjoyed. This was just the latest demonstration of his own intellectual and social deficiencies.

Instead, I recognized this as an opportunity to get not only some valuable diagnostic assistance; more important to me, it was a chance to get a different kind of "blue card."

I was given the Scholastic Aptitude Test (SAT) through the use of a reader, as well as certain temperament, or interest, tests. A few weeks later, I was given the Weschler Adult Intelligence Scale, one of two most respected, individually-given adult intelligence tests in use at the time.

Shortly after completing this test, I was invited into the office of Dr. Ferkins, the head of the Counseling and Testing Center at Texas Christian University. He began by telling me that I had scored so highly on the SAT that he and his staff thought I had cheated. However, now that they had administered the intelligence test, my score on the SAT looked believable.

Dr. Ferkins didn't tell me what my score had been on the SAT, but he did describe the results of the IQ test. I had scored somewhere in the top one or two percent of men 22 years of age—the highest scoring subgroup.

I had missed three vocabulary words: ominous, edifice, and impale. He even took the time to define each. As he completed this task, I began formulating a hypothesis about why I'd never heard such a strong assessment of my potential.

Dr. Ferkins told me that I should feel free to pursue *any* career, including one as a medical doctor or even a scientist. Given my sight limitations, this was no small praise and reinforced my long held assessment and, if possible, bolstered my self-esteem. At last, someone in an official capacity, using an official measurement, had seen what I had believed since my days in Mrs. Downs' class. Dr. Ferkins informed me that he would be sending a letter to my counselors at Tarleton. I couldn't have been happier, as that had been my primary goal for taking the initiative.

Needless to say, this event was very significant—another turning point in my life. Once the letters were received by my two faculty advisors, each of whom was a department head, my academic life took a decidedly different turn.

It quickly became obvious that the contents of these letters had been discussed widely among the faculty in the Department of Social Sciences. I received the highest grade in the class in courses taught by professors under whom I had previously received Ds. They had assumed because I wasn't a traditional student and because of the lack of resources I enjoyed when taking my first course under them that I wasn't very smart. My hope is that I instilled in them an appreciation that intelligence really is more than skin deep—that poor handwriting and spelling did not always mean what they had assumed.

It had been a long road, but I had managed to reverse the discrimination that I had experienced for almost my entire academic career.

I was scheduled to graduate in May of 1969, and despite my academic freedom, I almost didn't make it. My trigonometry instructor called me to his desk one afternoon to ask if I could see well enough to read the logarithmic tables in the back of the book. I realized the question was asinine since we both already knew the answer. The print was much smaller than the rest of the print in the book. At the beginning of the semester, I had carefully explained to him that I couldn't see the book whatsoever. All semester he had permitted me to take my tests on a chalkboard using a student grader to read me the problems and record my calculations on paper.

I attempted to explain how I could instruct the student grader as to the proper coordinates for finding the formula number. Once he would read me the number, I could work the problem.

Instead, the instructor announced that no one could pass his course without being able to read those tables for himself. Of course, not being domiciled in the Social Science Department, this professor knew nothing of my stunning score on the I.Q. test. Otherwise, he might have been concerned that his actions could come back to embarrass him. At any rate, he was one of very few professors I encountered who was just a jerk.

Enough was enough. Without a second's hesitation, I headed immediately for the office of the president of the college, whom I'd never met. I explained what had taken place. The president listened with complete interest and then began to write something on a piece of paper. I could hear the warmth in his voice as he handed me that sheet of paper. He told me to take it to the registrar's office. "This is a presidential waiver," he said with a smile. "You no longer have to have trig to graduate because I said so." I had never imagined such a thing, but I thanked him profusely and headed off to the registrar's office with a big smile on my face. I was ecstatic.

My ecstasy turned to angst when I learned that I would now be shy by two credit hours. This meant missing the May commencement, but after attending summer school, I graduated in August. Finally, I arrived with my parents for the graduation that I was never supposed to experience. As my parents and I arrived, Dr. Grant approached us and jokingly said in a satisfied tone, "I tried to tell you that day in Dean Conyus' office three years ago that you couldn't do this. You're blind." Actually, Dr. Grant may have harbored such a thought during that fateful first meeting, but he never said it out loud; I would certainly have remembered. What I cared about was his obvious pleasure at the outcome.

How appropriate it was and what joy it gave me that Dean Conyus delivered the commencement speech. He quoted from the Apostle Paul during his address. I had long identified with Paul more than any other personality in the Bible. Paul had a thorn in his flesh, just as I did. He too had understood what it meant to run a difficult race, keep the faith, and claim the prize.

CHAPTER 9

BIG CITY, BIG PLANS

After graduation, I returned to Mineral Wells, where I could live with my parents and look for work, since I had spent most of my money attending summer classes in order to graduate.

My old buddy, Ken Gruben, returned to Mineral Wells after a three-year stint in the Air Force and was planning on attending Texas A&M in the spring to complete his undergraduate degree. I was debating whether to follow my brother and attend law school at Texas Tech. I had indirectly received some encouragement to do so: the school was in the process of installing an elaborate accommodation for blind students, and the dean told my brother he would be interested in talking to me.

Jimmy felt that I would be a gifted trial attorney but would suffer a tremendous disadvantage in trying to search through, not to mention read, law books. He felt the challenge would be for me to get established enough to be designated by a firm as strictly a trial lawyer whose research would be done by others.

Instead, I decided to pursue a master's degree at Texas A&M University. Ken and I began to make plans to room together.

About a month into our planning, Mr. Jackman from the State Commission of the Blind showed up at my parents' home one day. I shared my plans to attend graduate school and asked about financial support through his organization. He said that my tuition would be paid as long as I attended a state-supported school, and I would be eligible to receive $130 per month in aid to the blind. This was great news—I had received just $78 a month when I turned 21 during my first year at Tarleton.

The $130 pretty much matched what my living expenses at Tarleton had been. My parents had to scrape together the difference between the $78 I received and the rest of my expenses, including tuition. I contributed by paying for my clothes and at least some of my books from money I earned during summer breaks.

There was no way I was going to ask my parents to subsidize my graduate work as well. It was 1969, and Dad was still driving the GMC pickup he had purchased in 1957. The increased stipend meant that I could make it without help from my parents.

Mr. Jackman shared one other piece of valuable information. He said that there was an eye doctor in Fort Worth who could fit people like me with a pair of glasses that would allow them to read normal print. It sounded like a gift from heaven, so I jumped at the opportunity.

Unlike most of my past visits to eye doctors, this one actually had some positive results. The doctor handed me a pair of glasses. These were not prescription glasses. Instead, one lens was nothing more than a very strong magnifying glass, and the other was frosted. The magnifying glass was about three-fourths of an inch thick, and it was so powerful that it focused at a distance of about one inch.

The doctor showed me a card containing a variety of print sizes, which ranged from large at the top of the card to very small at the bottom. I was able to read about a half-dozen lines, reading type I'd never been able to see before. I bought a pair right on the spot.

My investment of $53 plus tax represented nearly a week's wages, but more importantly it meant that, for the first time, I could read newspaper-size print. While not a panacea—the focal distance of one inch was too close to permit reading with both eyes (they would cross)—it was as if a whole new world opened up to me.

Unfortunately, my euphoria didn't last long: I had to do all reading with one eye, and hold my head at exactly the same distance from the reading surface. The greatest limitation concerned the small field of vision. I could only see 10 or 12 letters at one time, which made the process extremely slow. After I got used to my new glasses, Ken timed me—80 words per minute. Not exactly speed reading compared to others who could read up to 800 words per minute.

Still, having these glasses meant that I would be able to read test questions, decipher forms such as applications, and read short passages of text. When I got home, the first thing I picked up to read was a Bible. I began reading in Genesis, and by the time I got to the part about Methuselah, I realized that I would have to live at least as long as he did to ever finish the Bible at the rate I was going.

Since I was not in school when I purchased the glasses, I stored them in a safe place and focused on work and hung around with Ken. We made several trips to Fort Worth that fall, all of which included a stop at Cyclemart, a large Honda dealership with good prices. We both shared a love of motorcycles.

Like other guys in their 20s, we had champagne taste but didn't have a champagne budget. That didn't stop me from purchasing a bike that would offer me mobility and independence—the same feeling I had years ago when my parents bought me my first scooter.

What I really wanted was a Honda SL 175 dual-purpose bike, but it cost way more than I had or could afford. I chose a more affordable model, but needed some way to get it home. My friend Glenn Blankenship and I rented a U-Haul trailer and headed for Cyclemart. The new 1970 models were on the showroom floor, and the salesman said he would sell me a 1969 model for $30 less. I selected a blue bike.

As we arrived in Mineral Wells, we decided to turn in the trailer before delivering the bike to my parents' house. There was a back road that we could take, and the plan was for me to follow Glenn. I pulled into our driveway right behind Glenn.

My mother and sister Mary, now in the fourth grade, were virtually in tears. Although I was now 23, Mama seemed far more certain that I would kill myself than she had ever let on when I got my first bike 12 years earlier.

Before we had even finished lunch, Ken showed up. The three of us headed for the nearest dirt road, and I began to teach both of them how to ride a motorcycle. I was having the time of my life—I had forgotten how free being on a motorcycle made me feel. It's hard for someone with normal sight to understand the sense of freedom and control I got from riding my bike—even short distances.

I rode up and down the nearby country roads, which helped to relieve the awful sense of being stranded, a feeling I had come to associate with our house because it was so far from everything—and everyone. For the rest of the family, town was a pleasant three or four minutes away. For me, however, those few miles of gently rolling countryside were akin to the English Channel. They separated me from the rest of the continent. I always had to rely on someone to ferry me to the mainland. Nighttime had always been the worst. The ferry seldom ran at night, even though that was when I had the most free time.

I rarely rode my motorbike at night, and I almost never rode it into town. Regardless, I was aware of the dangers, and was always careful. While I considered town driving safer than highway driving because the slow rate of travel allowed for a greater response time, my main concern was that I would be stopped for a driver's license check. Unlike the two motorbikes I'd had as a child, this cycle required a driver's license I did not have—or ever would. However, it was a small price to pay for the freedom and independence I experienced. I didn't feel as blind on my bike as I did walking, or even reading. When I walked, I was always reminded of why I was walking—because I was visually impaired. When I rode my bike, I became more aware.

During this time, John Gresham, a friend from BSU who was teaching math at Texas Christian University (TCU) and working on his Ph.D. at the school, continued to live in nearby Stephenville, where his wife was finishing her degree. From time to time, John and Glenn would jump on his Honda and come to Mineral Wells to get me for a couple of days. Glenn would drive my bike to Stephenville and back while I rode behind John.

During these brief visits to Stephenville, we played Spades each night, all night. I had been the first of our group of friends to move away, so my return was always the impetus to get everyone together. With the old gang, no one seemed to care that I couldn't really see—I was the same as everyone else.

These gatherings were wonderful diversions from working, and being stranded at a house in the country. They provided a respite which helped that fall pass quickly. Each time we'd throw one leg across the seat and head back to Mineral Wells, I felt good. I looked forward to seeing my parents, Mary, and especially Janie.

Ken and I worked at the same company, and were laid off on the same day when the company announced financial difficulties. At the suggestion of my father, we both applied—and got hired—at Cantex, a factory that produced clay pipe. In those days, my visual impairment never seemed to get in the way of me finding a job—no doubt because they were not great jobs to begin with.

This work was fine, although Ken and I hadn't ever worked in such a large facility before. This was an enormous place that made me nervous because I not only had to keep my eyes open to the task at hand, I had to make sure I didn't get hurt. I was constantly focused on being careful and staying safe.

The large pipes measuring about two feet in diameter and 10 or 12 feet long were stacked about 15 to 18 feet high. Each pipe weighed at least several hundred pounds. There was always the danger that a stack would become dislodged, crushing whatever—or whoever—might be in the way.

Needless to say, this concerned me, particularly since the stacks were formed using forklifts, whose operators competed with each other to see how fast they could race outside the building to another area where the pipes were stored after firing.

While I was no doubt the employee with the poorest eyesight, after demonstrating that I could pay attention to the details, I got a job lubricating the joints, or bells, as they are sometimes called. While this job was considered dangerous by many, to me it was one of the safest in the factory.

With paintbrush and bucket of lube in hand, I would climb up the ends of two stacks of pipe, which were two or three feet apart. By putting my right foot in a pipe on one stack and my left in a pipe in the other stack, I could brace myself and use the arrangement as a makeshift ladder. It was quite a fall from the top, but what I cared most about was that the pipes would roll *away* from me in the event of a disaster. What I lacked in vision, I made up for in common sense.

. . .

When it was time for registration at Texas A&M, Ken and I got our things together and traveled to College Station in his white VW bug. Never having been there, I didn't know what to expect.

We found a no-frills motel near the campus, where we spent the night. The next morning, we awoke to a gorgeous balmy day. It was January 12, 1970, my sister Mary's 10th birthday. After breakfast, we checked out and headed for our first look at the campus.

Ken knew exactly what he wanted to major in—forestry. I was interested in pursuing an advanced degree in philosophy, but first I needed to gain admission as a graduate student, something I was confident would happen. Ken pointed me in the direction of the Academic building, a structure with a huge dome that reminded me of the state capitol in Austin. Ken had parked the car near the only water tower, a landmark I could see from far away. We agreed to meet back at the car by noon, and headed off in opposite directions.

Dr. Davenport, head of philosophy, explained that his department didn't offer a postgraduate degree and suggested Urban & Regional Planning instead. Although I didn't get the connection between philosophy and city planning, he seemed to think I should check it out. He gave me instructions for finding the Architecture building, which housed the Graduate College of Urban Planning.

Once I found my way to the Architecture building and the Department of Urban Planning, I met a very helpful graduate assistant, Ms. King. She worked in the office part-time and attended class as well. Her explanation of the program sounded like something that would interest me—Dr. Davenport was right. It sounded creative yet practical, and from what I could determine from talking to Ms. King, and from looking at samples of projects on display, wouldn't require a lot of close work or good eyesight.

It would require good reasoning and conceptual skills, so I decided to give it a go. Ms. King asked if I'd taken the Graduate Record Exam (GRE) and explained that it was required at Texas A&M.

"No," I said, and then I explained that I had arranged for and possessed a copy of the letter Dr. Ferkins had written about the results of my I.Q. test. She volunteered to take me to see the dean of admissions for graduate studies. The dean read the letter and examined a copy of my undergraduate transcript, which I also provided. He said that he was going to make an exception to the school's policy that no one be permitted to register for a full semester load without first having produced a satisfactory score on the GRE or having first completed a successful semester taking a lesser load. He asked me to promise him that I would take the exam later that spring and then authorized me to register.

Before long, it was official—I was enrolled as a student of urban planning. Ken and I met up, and then headed back to Mineral Wells.

When I arrived home and told my father the news that I was going to be a city planner, he was thrilled. Being a plumber and mechanical wizard, he clearly preferred the more tangible city planning to the more esoteric philosophy that I had intended to pursue. When my mother returned from church, I went out to the garage to see her in and tell her about my decision.

It was clear that she wasn't moved by my remarks. Sensing this, my father encouraged her to listen more attentively. "Mother," he said in a tone that conveyed the gentlest possible rebuke, "your son is trying to tell you what he is going to make of himself. He's going to be a city planner."

CHAPTER 10

GREAT EXPECTATIONS

Ken and I returned to College Station a couple of weeks later, arriving late one Saturday afternoon. We got a motel room and then grabbed supper. Tired from the long drive, we went back to our room and turned on the television. It seems like an odd thing to remember after so many years, but *The Andy Williams Show* was on, and he was singing a song I'd never heard before. Not surprisingly, it was a love song. What struck me most was the line, "Even told the golden daffodils."

In addition to savoring the richness of Andy's voice, the words he sang seemed to describe the sense of excitement and optimism that surpasses the literal. Despite the frustrations, challenges, and hurdles I have encountered, this philosophy was one that I have always embraced. I have always dared to expect the best out of life, despite being told over and over not to expect much. At that very moment, I felt more vindicated in my views than ever. Suddenly, it hit me: not only did I graduate from college, I was beginning graduate school—something the "pragmatists" had never imagined for me.

For as long as I could remember, it had been in my psyche to feel optimistic and reassured—most of the time. After everything I had accomplished so far, I had a right to feel as though I had caught a falling star and put it in my pocket. I felt a sense of accomplishment just being at Texas A&M.

After Andy signed off, Ken and I left the room and walked towards the car, parked just outside the door, to finish unloading it. When we got in, and turned on the radio, the song about the daffodil was playing, and once again Andy was singing about falling stars. Along with the glorious sunset at that moment, I took it as a sign of better things to come.

Although it was getting dark, we decided to drive around and check out apartment complexes near the north end of the campus. It was especially important for me to live close to campus and specifically, the Architecture building. Most of my classes would be held there, and I would have to walk to campus and back two or three times a day.

I also wanted to locate the BSU. The BSU and local Baptist churches had been such a great source of support to me while attending Weatherford College and Tarleton, so it was important for me to locate both first thing. BSU was where I had met many of my closest friends and girlfriends. Most of the people I had encountered at both BSU and church shared my values—they didn't swear or use derogatory language, and they respected women. I was drawn to group activities, including devotional meetings, social events, recreational activities, and Friday night trips to sing hymns at local nursing homes and missions. Singing was always one of my favorite activities, whether entertaining patients at a nursing home or just standing around a piano at the BSU. I knew most of the words to the songs by heart, and if I didn't, there was usually someone willing to read me the words before we began singing. Whether singing with the a cappella choir on campus or the sanctuary choir at church, I was able to memorize both words and music with relative ease.

Every roommate and every girl I had ever dated had been someone from either the BSU or church. I fully expected to meet my wife at one of these two venues. As luck would have it, Ken and I discovered not only the BSU but the First Baptist Church of College Station within the first block of the campus' main entrance at Old College Main Street. We spotted a few apartment complexes on College Main, as well as a brand new one about three-fourths of a mile from campus.

When we returned to check out apartments the next day, we kept running up against "no vacancy" signs. We decided to check out the new complex, figuring there would be plenty of vacancies there, given that there hadn't been that many cars in the still-unpaved parking lot the night before.

We were right. The rent was $145 per month—twice what I was paying at Tarleton, where I had three roommates. However, I bit the bullet and assumed I would make some friends who would end up becoming suitemates before the next semester. The location meant a three-mile round-trip to the Architecture building; fortunately, the BSU was centrally located between the apartment and the campus and would make a good waystation.

We paid a deposit and the first month's rent. As soon as we were finished, I headed to the BSU and Ken went off on his own. Ken had always been a loner. He was quiet, private—and brilliant. I had no desire to try to change the first two, and I would never have been able to change the third even if I wanted to. We simply accepted each other as-is and enjoyed each other as unique individuals.

I carefully chose my steps through the muddy parking lot and started down the narrow asphalt street in the direction of the BSU and the campus. The walk was inspiring because it represented both freedom and inclusion. I felt liberated from the isolation I grew up with living in the country.

The BSU was a 10-minute walk from our apartment. Even though it was Sunday afternoon, the doors were open. Inside, I was greeted by three young men, all students at the university: Keith Price, Sammy White, and Bill Riley. They immediately welcomed me and offered to show me around the building. From that moment on, I knew I would be at home at Texas A&M, and especially at the BSU. These three guys were typical of individuals I had met at the two previous BSUs and all shared my values. As evangelical Christians, they were eager to welcome people into an environment where the gospel was regularly taught. We talked about our majors, and when they realized I was the only graduate student, that seemed to add to my credibility and acceptability.

During the tour, Keith commented that I had come at a particularly quiet time, pointing out that there was just the four of us there. I was able to make out a ping-pong table and asked if we could play, given that no one else was around. Announcing I wanted to take on the best player among them, Keith stepped forward. Soon I discovered I was no match for him, despite my aggressive approach. I didn't disclose that I was legally blind until after we had played a few games—Keith, Sammy, and Bill were all shocked given my assertive performance. In fact, they seemed to think it was kind of cool.

After we finished, Keith told me about the center's programs, including a free devotional lunch each weekday. The churches in the association would each take turns providing lunch while someone, usually the BSU director, would give a devotional talk. He invited me to attend the lunches, as well as evening programs.

Before I knew it, it was late afternoon, and Keith needed to lock up before church services that evening. Walking back toward my apartment, I thought about the new friendships I had made at the BSU. I knew this was going to be a special place.

. . .

The next morning, February 4, 1970, marked the official start of the spring semester. For me, this was more than just the first day of a new semester. I was settling into a new life, on a new campus, and studying a subject I'd first learned of only a few weeks earlier. A new decade had just begun and I welcomed it with open arms. As it had been for so many other people, the 1960s had been a decade of tremendous struggle. I felt like a critically ill patient who had been given a new lease on life. I knew I had overcome the odds, but I also knew I couldn't settle, or I would end up reliving the anxiety of the past.

Classes in the Department of Urban Planning were held only on Tuesdays, Wednesdays, and Thursdays to facilitate out-of-town trips to work on projects. Since I essentially had my first day off, I headed for the BSU. I was anxious to see it in full swing, make more new friends, and take in the devotional lunch.

When I walked in, I spied an open office door with a woman sitting behind a desk—when she saw me, she stopped typing, invited me to sit down, and then introduced herself as Toni Massey. She went on to explain that she was the part-time secretary/assistant director for the BSU. She was warm and easy to talk to, and a steady stream of students came in and out of her office as we were speaking. It felt comfortable—kind of like a kid strolling through mama's kitchen. Like Toni, each person was warm and friendly when she introduced them. Just as at Weatherford and Tarleton, I adopted the BSU as my home away from home—my lifeline.

The next day I attended my first urban planning classes. Located on the third floor of the Architecture building, we sat around a huge conference table in front of an equally impressive window that overlooked the main entrance to the campus.

Needless to say, I couldn't see the full distance to the campus' main entrance, Eastgate, because it was about a third of a mile away. I could make out the end of the tree-lined boulevard and enjoyed watching cars as they approached, entered, and were turned onto the beautiful loop which circled the easternmost buildings, including our own. We all felt as if we were seated at the academic center of the universe—underscored by the credentials of our instructors, including degrees from MIT, Harvard, and Notre Dame. I knew I would not be disappointed.

During our lunch break, I headed for the devotional luncheon at the BSU, feeling I was part of something special. During the devotional message, I became preoccupied with my first morning of classes. It's hard to describe how I felt at that particular moment, other than to say there was a profound sense of fulfillment at having overcome so many obstacles to arrive at this point.

Late that afternoon I returned to the apartment, rejoicing in the fulfillment I felt after my first day of classes. After a quick dinner and recap with Ken, I headed out to attend the evening devotional at the BSU. This was the first of many trips I would make at night, walking alone down the scarcely traveled road. Most of the way was well lit, but the portion which passed through an undeveloped swampy creek bottom was not. It would have been a challenge with normal vision—for me, one slip could spell disaster.

Generally speaking, I didn't encounter many cars, but the ones that came towards me blinded me and made my already dismal sight worse. The occasional car that would approach from behind would bring needed light but I risked getting hit. Since there were no sidewalks along most of the road, I would end up waiting until a car got fairly close and then stepped into the borrow ditch. Needless to say, these ditches were not the most pedestrian friendly places to walk. But given the choice of standing in the path of oncoming cars or moving to the borrow ditch, I chose the latter. It was—literally—a balancing act.

On those nights when I returned late, the walk back was even more unnerving because the road was basically abandoned, which could have made me vulnerable to mischief from passersby. However, I took comfort in knowing that my size and build would tend to discourage such a thing. Besides, it was pretty obvious I was a college student who probably didn't have two nickels to rub together. At any rate, to me it was worth the risk because of the friends I had made at the BSU. Three nights each week, there was a brief devotional message that attracted a large group of students. Afterwards, a contingent would hang around the center. I enjoyed this time enormously. Almost every person I met was easy to talk to and kind towards me.

One evening, just about time for the devotional to begin, I was in the library at the BSU looking at magazines and reading an occasional large-print caption, when I noticed a young woman enter at the opposite end of the room. Although I was too far away to see her clearly, the vague image of her that I could discern was enough to make me jump up and go introduce myself. The closer I got, the more stunning she became. Somehow, I managed to state my name correctly and learned that her name was Susan. She was about 5 feet 2 and petite with shoulder-length black hair, powerful brown eyes, and lovely features. Within a span of about 90 seconds, I was smitten. All I could think about was not blowing this opportunity to make a favorable impression, which, of course, is exactly what I did. Perhaps for the first time in my adult life, I was tentative and unsure of myself. At that moment, I stopped being myself and began to fear that if I offered to accompany her into the meeting room, I might do something awkward because of my poor eyesight. That fear was totally unfounded in reality. Ordinarily, I was as sure-footed as a tom cat and twice as confident. But this was different.

It didn't help that my three years at Tarleton had failed to produce a single relationship that lasted longer than a couple of months, with most ending after two or three dates. Certainly, I had terminated my share of these—usually because the level of conversation was not very stimulating. When that was not the case, I often sensed there was something else at work. At one point, I wondered if I was just not physically attractive enough. The thought that anyone who knew me very well at all could think my limited eyesight would keep me from being successful was inconceivable to me. But, I was naive. Near the end of my time at Tarleton, a coed I had known throughout my stay there motioned for me to follow her out to the steps near the sidewalk in front of the BSU and away from other students. She was very attractive, but I had always thought her shallow. However, what she said that day changed my assessment and endeared her to me. She said, "Walter, I want to let you know what is going on around here. Please allow me to explain it from my own situation. I think you are really, really smart and will earn $30,000 a year some day." That was a pretty bold prediction, since the average American family was earning about $6,000 annually at that time. "Here is the problem: my parents are just staying together until we kids get out of college. I am the oldest, and I am expected to graduate as soon as possible and get a job, so I can help. I need to marry someone who can help in a big way and quickly." These were unusual words coming from someone I had never dated and was not trying to date at the time. This young woman cared enough to say something that took courage to say. Then as now, I considered what she did to rate among the greatest acts of friendship I received while at Tarleton. She had the courage to tell me that because I had trouble seeing, that girls were not responding to me the way they might respond to someone "normal." She was upfront enough to tell me that she had to marry someone who was not disabled—and that was probably the case with other girls on campus.

Unfortunately, the memories of that day were rattling around in my sub-conscious when I was trying to make an appropriate response to Susan.

The devotional program was already underway in another part of the building, which prompted my new acquaintance to say, "I don't know if I should go in there."

I started to say, "I'd march in there like I owned the place if I looked like you," but lost my nerve and omitted the compliment at the end. My response ended up sounding egotistical, at least to me. Even worse, it could have been taken as though I was "dismissing her." Of course, it could have been taken several ways, but I felt like I had blown my opportunity to make the right impression—the whole experience should have never happened because that was the first time I had ever failed to join in on the devotional. For some inexplicable reason, I just did not want to that evening. Had I done what I had always done, our relationship would likely have gotten off to a better start. Fortunately, I had learned during our brief encounter that she lived with her parents in College Station, and that they were all active members of the First Baptist Church. This information indicated to me that she was much more than an attractive girl with a great personality; she almost surely shared my values. At any rate, she went off into the meeting by herself, and I didn't see her again that night after the meeting was over.

Over the next few days, I spent a lot of time at the BSU, hoping Susan would drop by so our conversation could resume. Little did I know she had a strong emotional reason to avoid the place. Her old boyfriend, who had recently moved out of state, and the BSU director were best friends. After a week or two, I couldn't stand it anymore and decided to call her for a date. Because she lived off campus, I had to deal with the issue of my inability to drive. I looked around the BSU for a couple we could double-date with, and then called her and asked her out. When the big night came, I got a call from the couple telling me they were running very, very late. This immediately caused me to feel embarrassed and reduced my confidence. From that point on, any time I was around Susan, I felt tense, and that feeling transferred to her. We were attracted to each other but there was always that wall of tension between us. There was a series of unfortunate events that didn't help, and we ended up going our separate ways. However, I now realize that as bad as I felt then, the Lord was answering my prayers by actively blocking the relationship as part of His plan. Certainly, if He were blocking the relationship it was not because there was anything wrong with Susan.

About the time the wheels were coming off my relationship with Susan, a train wreck unfolded in my academic life. Just as my early days at Weatherford College and Tarleton had been characterized by frustration, disappointment, and humiliation, so it was at A&M. I soon learned that urban planning students were expected to complete a major study with exhibits and recommendations at the end of fall and spring semesters. Because I began at midterm, as did Jesus Hinajosa, the instructor who would be supervising my project, neither of us knew what to expect at semester's end. The other students were already ensconced in teams formed earlier in the year. Not able to join a team midstream, I struck out on my own and decided to do a study of the Central Business District (CBD) in my hometown, Mineral Wells. This seemed logical as Ken and I planned to go home for the weekend at least a couple of times during the semester. Unfortunately, Ken's car was rear-ended, and its engine trashed. I now had no way of getting to Mineral Wells to conduct the research for my project until there was barely time to make preliminary notes and sketches, and no way to construct anything more than a single, crude, and preliminary graphic. Professor Hinajosa understood that my hands were largely tied and that more time would be required to complete the project properly. When the day came for me to present a status report and gain direction, a formal architectural jury was assembled by the department head, Professor McGraw. He assembled a group of instructors, including some I had never met. Not having come into the urban planning program from an architectural background as roughly one-half of my classmates had done, I had never heard of an architectural jury. What happened next can best be described as a verbal water cannon, trained on me. There were voices I did not recognize, all hurling insults at me. Just as surely as I knew virtually nothing about some of these folks, they knew nothing about me, and understandably could not get their heads around the severity of my sight loss, transportation issues, and other challenges. These were not mean people—in fact, quite the contrary. They were just responding to perceptions that were all wrong. They assumed I wasn't taking my studies seriously.

The teams who came before and after me all included members who were experts in preparing beautiful graphics because they had been doing that through five years of undergraduate study. After 15 to 20 minutes of group target practice aimed at pointing out my numerous deficiencies, I was as spent as the metaphorical shell casings that shared the floor with me. Finally, Professor McGraw said, "We are not really here just to shovel shit on you." I remember thinking, "You could have fooled me!" Then he asked if I believed Professor Hinajosa had failed to prepare me properly. What was I supposed to say? There was no way I could afford to throw him under the bus. He seemed as caught off guard as I was about the ensuing carpet bombing. Moreover, at that moment, I considered him one of only two friends I had on the faculty. Finally, it was agreed that I needed more time to complete the project which, ironically, is exactly how I had begun my remarks.

Being made to appear far less intelligent and less focused than I was was an outgrowth of my visual circumstances. Shaking off the crap and finding a work-around is what I had always done and was what I would do this time. To formulate a workable plan, I had first to understand why I had been selected as the chick at the bottom of the pecking order. The obvious answer was that I had truly appeared weak. The second and closely related factor was that I had not yet found a way to let these people see me as bright, let alone gifted. In contrast to the situation at Tarleton, where key professors received a letter making it clear that I had a genius I.Q., the faculty of the Department of Urban Planning had received nothing except the results of my performance on the Graduate Record Exam (GRE). Because 800 of the possible 1,600 points came from the single subject of math, I was at a big disadvantage. While I was very good at stated problems and quantitative thinking in general, I lacked exposure to the more esoteric forms of math. A second factor was that the arbitrary allotment of time set at twice that for normally sighted students proved problematic. Providing twice as much time for people to read at one-fourth the speed at which other gifted students could read for themselves just didn't work. For example, the verbal half of the exam contained lengthy passages that had to be read aloud in order to answer very detailed questions about content and concepts. Despite having exceptional listening and retention skills, the inability to spot-check facts by quickly scanning materials once read proved a significant handicap. Despite these and other biases built into the exam and testing procedure, I did manage to score in the 63rd percentile when compared to other graduate students studying within the broad discipline of architecture. While this score was certainly acceptable, it was not high enough to positively impact the attitudes of relevant players in the Department of Urban Planning and prevent the attacks from the architectural jury.

To redeem myself, and enhance my image within the Urban Planning Department, I would have to overcome a very rocky beginning and my lackluster score on the GRE. During the first six weeks of summer, I spent considerable time in Mineral Wells, gathering information useful in picking up the broken pieces of my Central Business District study. To achieve this, I decided to interpret the term "Reader Service" rather broadly. For purposes of paying folks to help me complete the project, I billed the State Commission for the Blind for hours spent driving me to and around the study sites I defined "Reader Services" to include reading the names off buildings and street signs and snapping pictures of the study area. Before long, I earned credit for a satisfactory project. I also figured out how to avoid another ugly experience before an architectural jury: I would attach myself to a team where my part would be small, and someone else could prepare the graphics.

Similar to my early experiences at Weatherford College and Tarleton—characterized by a lack of essential tools which led to frustration, disappointment, and even humiliation—my start at A&M had been rocky. As with the earlier venues, I managed to overcome the setbacks and spend the remainder of my time positively. As before, the message of just how limited my eyesight really was and how strong my determination and ability were did not come across at first.

Happily, an opportunity to change perceptions within the department came that summer. One day we watched a film, but Professor Gardner, who was team teaching a course with Jesus Hinajosa, was absent. When he returned the next day, he inquired about the movie. Immediately, I volunteered to brief him and gave a very detailed account. My description sounded more like a courtroom reporter reading yesterday's testimony than a thumbnail sketch of the basics. The responses that followed made it clear that I had helped the two professors and surrounding classmates see me in a much more favorable light.

As I began redeeming myself in the Department of Urban Planning, something unrelated and wonderful happened. My personal fortunes improved in a life-changing way. On June 10, 1970, I caught my first glimpse of a young woman entering the BSU; she was about 10 feet ahead of me, and I had never seen her before.

That evening, my new summer-school suitemates, Randy Cook, Charles Jamison, Gary Mayfield, and I were talking about this new young lady. Randy had already met her and was impressed at learning that she had already earned a degree and taught school for three years—despite being just 23. It didn't hurt that she was extremely attractive. Pretty soon a controversy arose—the color of her dress. Yes, guys talk about this stuff as well. One of the guys said it was blue; another, green. I interrupted with a grin and said, "I think you are both blind; that girl was wearing an orchid dress. I just hope one of you did a better job of getting her name." "It's Gail Jones," said Randy. Obviously, she had made quite an impression on him, as he had already gathered a number of facts by visiting with her. This seemed curious since he already had a girl-friend, who often appeared with him at the BSU. For this reason, I did not see Randy as a competitor for her affections. That was probably a good thing; otherwise, I might have talked myself into defeat as I had done with Susan. As it happens, Randy was quite good-looking, could play the guitar, and sing like Johnny Cash. Also, he was a mechanical engineer who was smart and had a killer smile. I had been wrong to assume he had no romantic interest in Gail. In fact, he took her out a time or two.

The day after chatting with my suitemates, I shared with Gail our conversation about her dress as a way of introducing myself. She said that I had been right about the color of her dress. Soon, I felt a comfort in talking to Gail, which allowed me to be myself. For that reason, our relationship began with an ingredient I had never injected into the earlier ones—I paid her a compliment. My whole focus shifted to one centered on making her feel accepted and admired rather than worrying about how my disability would come across. At long last, I had learned my lesson. Rather than just thinking complimentary thoughts, I actually gave voice to them. It worked. Sitting next to her before, during, and after the devotional and the peanut butter and jelly sandwiches, I had time to recover from the initial intimidation that hit me upon seeing her face up close for the first time. Because I had to be within three or four feet of someone to see their face clearly, I had virtually no time to collect myself before having to introduce myself. Gail was just the third or fourth girl I had met who elicited this feeling of intimidation at first glance. She had dark red hair—not the carrot-top variety—but the classy, thick, and perfectly in place type. Her eyes were a bright blue against her fair complexion. I noticed her high cheekbones and warm smile. By then, I was on my way to falling in love. Rather quickly, the strong social skills she had no doubt honed during her three years of interacting with the parents of first graders put me at ease.

From the very beginning, she was easy to talk to and fun to be with. I found her comfortable to be around. Our relationship was spontaneous, something I had not always enjoyed in the past. We began spending every spare minute together. From the time I first offered her a ride on my little blue Honda motorcycle, which, by this time, I had managed to get transported to College Station, conversation just flowed effortlessly between us. We both knew what we wanted, and pretty soon knew we had found it. Each of us would complete a master's degree in about a year and should thus be in relatively good financial shape to start a household. We seemed to draw closer together each day. After 20 days and evenings together, I proposed marriage, and she accepted. Just how quickly and naturally our relationship had developed was surprising to both of us. Although I had been attracted to Gail the first time I saw her up close, for me, it was not a matter of love at first sight—but love at first conversation. Unlike my encounter with Barbara Mikles seven years earlier, no dream foretold my initial meeting with Gail. Moreover, this time, my inability to drive a car did not prevent my asking for a date. This time, I didn't feel compelled to neutralize the "Big Negative"—the fact that I was permanently and severely sight-impaired. Now I was a successful graduate student.

Perceptions about me had changed since I was in high school. Back then, few of my classmates and even fewer of my teachers ever suspected I possessed exceptional intellectual gifts. By contrast, many who knew Gail and me through such informal groups as the BSU, Sunday school, or my suitemates, often spoke of my intellect in glowing terms.

Now that the true identity of the future Mrs. Walter Ashby had been settled in my mind, it was perhaps as good a time as any to try to make sense of that dream so long ago that seemed to announce Barbara Mikles as the woman the Lord had for me. By the time of this reflection, Barbara had been married to someone else for a half dozen years and had a son. What had gone wrong about regarding this dream? Three possible explanations eventually surfaced: (1) Sometimes Christians have strong impressions that seem to originate from the Lord, but do not. (2) The astonishing similarities between the girl in the dream and how and where I met Barbara were nothing more than very unlikely coincidences. (3) The dream was from the Lord, and the person in that dream really was Barbara Mikles. Meeting her and considering her so special changed the course of my life. This was the explanation that made the most sense to me. There was nothing specific about the dream that amounted to a promise that she was the girl I was supposed to marry, although that was the conclusion I reached at the time. In my judgment, Barbara Mikles was more beautiful than Jacqueline Kennedy, and the last time I had looked in the mirror, John Kennedy's face was not staring back at me. Why would a girl like that be interested in me? I believe the Lord wanted me to answer that question. He wanted me to look deep within myself and find the potential to distinguish myself by achieving noble purposes. When I took that long introspection, I decided to claim a measure of the brilliance that was so evident in my father. Moreover, I soon came to realize the most promising outlet for such gifts would be in written and spoken language. Certainly, these realizations would not come from the school's administrative staff, and only a handful of teachers had recognized above-average ability in me. Ironically, the lofty aspirations Barbara caused me to uncover meant I had no business marrying anyone for six or seven years after we met—years spent constructing the educational foundation that would be required. To complete the irony, I now found myself in a position to propose marriage to a very special young woman who had already distinguished herself in her chosen field, and to believe I could offer her a rewarding life.

Soon after our engagement, Gail called her mom in Midland to share the big news. She described me as 6 feet 4, a graduate student, very smart, and legally blind. Her mom's immediate reaction was to instruct Gail not to tell any of the family. When Gail shared this information with me, I figured her mom planned to talk her out of marrying me. A few days later, we headed to Midland for an extended July 4 weekend. My accompanying Gail would have two purposes. It would make the 800-mile round trip safer for Gail by having me with her, and it would give me a chance to meet her mom and brother. We arrived just as supper was about ready, and Gail's brother, Dick, met us at the door. Gail had told me that Dick was heavy but agile and extremely strong. I first saw him standing in the front door, turned slightly to one side because his shoulders were wider than the door opening. He reminded me of a Russian weightlifter, only friendlier. His hair was black and he weighed roughly three times what his sister weighed. Other than that, different hair color, and skin tone, they could have passed for twins. From there, it was on to the kitchen to meet Mrs. Jones. Gail had warned me that her mom's hair had turned snow white shortly after Mr. Jones had passed very suddenly two years earlier. He had just turned 47 and had never been diagnosed with heart disease. One evening, while at home, he got up to go to the bathroom and suffered a massive heart attack and died before reaching the hospital. Mrs. Jones, just 50 years old when I met her that evening, showed signs of the trauma she had endured and the strain of the responsibilities that fell to her. Dick was a high school senior when his dad passed and still lived at home. Gail, on the other hand, was 21 and teaching in El Paso. A few months later, when the school year ended, Gail secured a teaching job in Midland at a school near her mom's house, so she could live with her. For the next two years, Gail was with her mom constantly, until she entered graduate school at A&M a month earlier. The plan was for Gail and Dick to share an apartment in the fall when he would return there to resume his studies at the outset of his junior year. Within a matter of three or four weeks, I had staked a claim on Gail for life.

Despite all that was fear-inducing about me, Mrs. Jones, who has always preferred to be called Mama, pronounced Mam-maw, could not have been any more cordial, and the same was true for Dick. There can be little doubt that telltale signs of my limited vision surfaced, although I was not aware of anything awkward that transpired. As it happened, Gail and I returned just four weeks later to attend her cousin's wedding. While we were there, Mrs. Jones talked to Gail in private in an attempt to get her to break it off with me. Mrs. Jones painted a pretty bleak picture of Gail's financial prospects if she married me. Gail became upset and told me I would have to ride back to

College Station with a fellow classmate who happened to be in Midland that weekend. Needless to say, my trip back to College Station was not a happy one. A few days later, I visited with Gail and told her I was not surprised she had misgivings about marrying me. With that, I said I'd be easy to find if she decided she wanted to resume the relationship. Since early adulthood, I knew that I wanted a girl who believed in me wholeheartedly. I figured time would tell. Within a few days, we were back together.

From that point on, developing my relationship with Gail became the most important accomplishment and the most enjoyable aspect of my time at A&M, even more so than realizing my academic dreams; every minute alone with Gail was heavenly. For one thing, she demonstrated more creativity than any girl I had known. She was fascinating to talk to and very smart in a way that was new to me. She had not been a brilliant undergraduate student who was stellar in every academic subject, but had the most interesting insights and would blossom as a postgraduate student, where she could focus on her passion—elementary education and teaching kids to read. After summer school and the first long semester, Gail was selected to receive a graduate assistantship, which provided a small salary. In that capacity, she discovered a new device that could be amazingly helpful to me. It was the first cassette tape recorder I had ever seen. What is more, it offered a feature that would allow the listener to adjust the speed at which recorded materials could be played. Her department head and director of the Reading Lab, Dr. Ilika, sat down with us one day for an experiment. To begin with, Dr. Ilika played recorded textbook materials at normal speed. Then, little-by-little, he increased the speed to more than 400 words per minute, more than twice the normal rate. Surprisingly, I could understand every word and even found it easier to stay focused than listening at a normal rate. Both Dr. Ilika and Gail said it sounded like Donald Duck to them, but my listening skills were highly developed. Immediately, I wanted one of those little darlings, and not one having only playback capability but the recording feature as well. I called my long-time detractor at the State Commission for the Blind to inquire about getting such a device. He allowed that the State Commission did have a few cassette recorders but it was out of the question for me to get one for my personal use. My next call went to the President Protempore of the state senate, John Roy Creighton. He was from my hometown and was acquainted with my family, living scarcely a mile down the road from my parents. I got right through to him, and he told me that he would make a call or two. Within the hour, the Commission had managed to locate a cassette recorder for me and would be putting it in the mail to me that day. This device arrived in time for me to put it to good use as the semester, my last, drew to a close. For the first time ever, I could hire someone to record assigned materials while I was in a class somewhere, and I could listen to it at my convenience. Not only that, but I could easily rewind the tape to listen once again to something I did not understand the first time or just to help me focus on information and fix it in my mind. This device came late in my time at A&M, but proved especially helpful to me because I had shifted my coursework to a more aggressive level. The cassette recorder was a godsend.

. . .

Early on, I had gained special permission from the dean of the graduate school to take exceptionally large course loads, which enabled me to earn my master's in Urban Planning in 15 months rather than the customary two years. After completing the core courses in urban planning, I devoted all of my electives toward a second master's in Educational Psychology and Counseling, which fascinated me. Learning about how people learn was of great interest to me, and counseling addressed the desire I had harbored to help others since my early experiences with my sister Janie. Just how such diverse fields of study might result in a career was unclear. However, one morning I checked the mail and realized the question of which path to follow had pretty much been settled for me. I got a letter from the graduate dean, saying, "You can either go ahead and receive your master of Urban Planning Degree in May, or reject it and finish the remaining requirements for an M.A. in Educational Psychology in August, but you cannot have both." Eager to use the summer to find a job and prepare for marriage to Gail in August, I took the former.

The decision was a surprisingly easy one. I had planned all along to be a city planner, and I was not about to forfeit that degree. Moreover, I was eager to get through, get out, and get on with life. Because of my disability, I had always been a person with a sense of urgency, and that sense was especially keen in the spring of 1971. I was 25 years old and ready to start my career.

CHAPTER 11

MIDLAND

The sky was still black that mid-May morning when Gail drove me to the Greyhound bus station in Bryan. Since she had a teaching position awaiting her in her hometown of Midland—a town named for its location midway between El Paso and Fort Worth—we had decided that I would spend my summer there staying with her mother while looking for a job.

Gail, along with her brother, was staying behind to attend summer school. Doing this would allow Gail to finish her master's degree. Gail and I planned to marry after she was finished with grad school, but before she started teaching.

As the bus pulled away from the station, my mind raced. I was sad at leaving what I consider the best place I'd ever known. Leaving my fiancé was, in many ways, a metaphor for my leaving Texas A&M—it was a place I had come to love like no other. I took comfort in knowing I would be taking the grandest nugget I had found as I fled this treasure chest: Gail would be joining me for life in just a few months.

I also owned a new key to another treasure chest, in the form of my master's degree: Walter D. Ashby, master of Urban & Regional Planning.

Then came the more sobering question: would others now see me as they had not been able to see me before I had my master's degree? Would prospective employers and colleagues see me as not only independent, but as a potential leader? Or would they treat me as others had—disabled instead of enabled?

More than anything else, however, I thought about getting through the ordeal of a 14-hour bus ride. I had always hated bus trips, because they were nothing but cruel reminders of my not being able to drive. The abject inconvenience of having to spend 14 hours to go somewhere that would only take someone else seven or eight hours by car continued to frustrate me.

However, most of all, I thought about the situations that might take place during the journey, all of which required me to be able to see. I dreaded coping with bus stops. Something as simple as searching for a restroom or buying a snack at an unfamiliar lunch counter could result in disaster—what others didn't give a second thought to, I stressed about for hours. I was always concerned I would board the wrong bus and end up in Chicago or somewhere else.

Finally, after the double-decker had made its last stop and I managed to survive, I breathed a sigh of relief at having cleared the last obstacle. I could finally relax and contemplate what lay ahead. I thought of what it would be like to spend the summer as a guest in Mrs. Lillian Jones' home.

The urban planner in me pondered long-term, philosophical issues as I approached the city that would soon become my new home. However, at this particular point in time, I was more concerned about building a good relationship with my future mother-in-law and finding a job.

Long after I grew weary of the bus ride, we finally arrived in Midland. Gail's mother was waiting for me at the station. We went straight to her house, where I unpacked while she finished making us supper. She suggested that we go play miniature golf after we ate. This warm reception let me know I was going to like Mrs. Jones. And that we would have a pleasant summer together.

The consideration that Mrs. Jones extended to me that evening was indicative of the summer ahead. I made it a point to do everything possible to help out around the house by keeping the lawn mowed and edged, vacuuming and cleaning the house, polishing cabinets and helping with whatever chores I could. I considered this the least I could do to compensate her for my room and board. This arrangement worked out well for both of us: I had a place to stay and home-cooked meals, and she had someone to help take care of the house and yard.

I believe that it was God's plan that the two of us have that summer without Gail so we could get to know each other. Getting to know me as a person of ability with a strong work ethic helped relieve much of her anxiety and predispositions towards me.

I pursued any job lead I could get my hands on, and pretty much did whatever I needed to do to make interviews happen. Several times per week I would walk to town to visit the Texas Employment Commission and meet with any possible employers. This trip involved roughly an eight-mile walk. Sometimes I would catch a ride with Mrs. Jones, when she was either leaving for work in the morning or returning home in the evening.

Not only was I looking for a professional position, I was looking for odd jobs—anything to make money. After almost two months, I did land a job as a night watchman. Yes, a night watchman.

The owner of a local night watchman company landed a last-minute contract to guard a large, new, manufactured housing factory and ended up shorthanded. He was looking for someone physically intimidating who could discourage potential vandals. I got the job.

About the time I started at the plant, Gail and her brother came home for a mid-semester break. Dick stayed in Midland for the balance of the summer, but Gail had to return to campus and complete her master's.

While she was home, I continued to work, earning enough to pay for my portion of our wedding expenses. The graveyard shift I was on meant there wasn't much going on: Dick would bring his car to the plant so I could drive and at least get to feel the independence of driving a car. There was a chain-link fence surrounding the entire complex, and the gates were locked. I didn't have to worry about any other moving vehicles, and the car's headlights made it possible for me to stay in the driving lane. I generally drove at roughly walking speed, and there was a bright spotlight attached to the car which I was able to shine in every direction. Besides wanting to feel the freedom that came with driving a car, its presence dissuaded potential intruders.

As our wedding approached, I quit my job. Shortly before the big day, the Tarleton gang arrived to serve as my wedding party. The night before the wedding, they gave me a bachelor party and tormented me incessantly. It was wonderful. It made me appreciate how important friendships are—these guys had all been with me since my darkest days at Tarleton. Even though I was the only one with a disability, they had always treated me just like one of the guys.

All the rehearsing before our wedding failed to prepare me for what was ahead. Weddings had always been emotional events for me, but my own proved especially moving. I stood and watched as Gail made her way to the altar, accompanied by her brother, Richard. The closer she came, the better I could see how beautiful she looked.

When she stood right beside me, I felt the full emotional impact of what was happening. As I gazed at her, I thought about the fact that her marrying me was a complete leap of faith on her part. There I stood—legally blind and without a job, and she still chose to spend the rest of her life with me. To say I was humbled would be an understatement.

More than ever, I was determined to validate her faith and love by becoming successful. Years later, when I was the recipient of a major award, she shared with me something that helped me understand the full impact of that day: "The reason I married you was because I thought you were going to do great things, and I didn't want to miss out on that."

CHAPTER 12

BREAKING THE BARRIER

Once Gail and I returned from our honeymoon in Albuquerque, New Mexico, I picked up where I had left off in my search for a job. As I had done all summer, I hit the job search trail—on foot.

From our new home, the walk downtown was somewhat shorter, only about six miles round-trip versus the eight I'd made so many times from Gail's mother's house. As I had done before, I always checked in at the Texas Employment Commission, even though it never amounted to anything. My philosophy to try anything that might work as many times as necessary hadn't changed.

It was 1971, and Midland's economy was in the same protracted slump that had begun in the late 1950s. As a result, housing was dirt cheap. In fact, several hundred FHA-owned houses had just been removed from the city in order to be sold elsewhere. We are not talking about mobile homes; these were traditional brick veneered structures. The ultimate feast or famine city, Midland had always reflected the boom or bust fortunes of the oil and gas business. During and immediately following World War II, oil prices were relatively strong. By 1956, the price per barrel stood at roughly $3, $35-$40 in 2016 dollars. Unfortunately, it stayed that way for 17 years. While most everything else in the world inflated, including to some degree well servicing and drilling costs, oil did not. Oil companies laid off workers and did not replace those lost to attrition. Young adults left the area to attend college and never returned. The town had already lost population from its high, when white residents left the city, leaving what had been a more racially diverse area to one predominately Hispanic and African-American. There is no doubt that at least some of the white flight was racially motivated, but much of it was simply opportunistic—you could get more for your money a little further out. To me, there was a certain poetic justice in the flight to the west and north parts of town, as racial minorities and poor whites were able to acquire much better housing at very affordable prices.

Despite the town's economic woes, Gail and I felt that we were the beneficiaries of good fortune: we both felt the Lord brought us to Midland because Gail had a good teaching job waiting for her and housing was so reasonably priced. We both needed to work, and it made sense to search for one job rather than two. Also, we knew that a new regional planning commission was being formed with its headquarters to be located at the airport situated midway between Midland and Odessa.

I believed I would have an excellent chance of getting a job with the commission when it opened, since my master's degree was in urban and regional planning from Texas A&M, one of the premier planning schools in the Southwest. Convinced there was a great career opportunity for me there and believing the work of the commission was important, I focused on doing whatever I could to prepare for the opportunity that would likely come my way.

During my four-mile walk from Mrs. Jones' house to downtown, I had occasionally taken a break to visit County Judge Barbara Culver. Gail's mom worked in the same building where Judge Culver's husband, John, had his business. Barbara became an attorney as an outgrowth of reading to John during his stint in law school after his vision began to decline sharply. Like me, John was legally blind. After practicing law for several years, John followed his passion for collecting coins and turned it into a successful business. While reading lengthy legal documents was exhausting, he was able to look at one coin at the time using a magnifying glass for hours on end. Needless to say, Judge Culver had an exceptional understanding of what I was experiencing. She was also one of the founding officers of the Permian Basin Regional Planning Commission, the region that was hiring a planner. Not only was she on the board as an officer, she was unquestionably one of its strongest leaders. A natural leader, she would later serve a term on the Texas Supreme Court.

At Judge Culver's suggestion, I met with another judge in Lamesa, Texas. Judge Pratt was the county judge, and president of the planning commission's board. Just as they do now, connections count when you're looking for a job.

I took complete advantage of Judge Culver's assistance, and she was happy to help.

I applied for the first position up for grabs at the planning commission: executive director. For a 25-year-old to apply for such a position was bold, but for a legally blind, 25-year-old, newly-minted graduate with no real experience was especially audacious. However, I was then, and remain today, incurably confident in myself. What I lacked in sight I made up for in confidence. Had I not possessed this trait, I would likely have been marginalized. It was more survival than it was ego.

Many people expect those of us with disabilities to be timid and nonassertive. We are expected to "know our place"—and not be aggressive or reach for the stars. I learned that I was the only candidate who possessed a postgraduate degree in urban and regional planning. I also learned that the board was looking for someone with at least some municipal experience and were considering Ernie Crawford, the assistant city manager of Odessa.

While a little disappointing, it came as no surprise to me that Ernie got the job. Ernie was the obvious choice and proved very adept in this largely political position. Next up was the position of director of planning, a key technical post. I acted on an idea that Gail and I discussed one night—I don't remember which one of us came up with it, but it was pure genius, so it probably came from her. I have no doubt the Lord was also involved.

The next day, I set up an appointment with Ed McGruder, Midland's mayor. When we met that afternoon, I explained my interest in working for the planning commission. The mayor told me the commission would need someone with my technical training, and that it might be in Midland's interest to have one of its own at the commission. He contacted a councilman to get his input.

I listened anxiously to Mayor McGruder's part of the conversation, and it soon became clear that the two men agreed that I should get the job. After hanging up, he let me know that he would recommend me to Judge Culver. Within a few days, I had an interview scheduled with Ernie, in his new capacity as the executive director.

Between that time and my meeting with Ernie, something wonderful happened. Bill Merretta, my new counselor with the State Commission for the Blind, arranged for me to travel to Houston to visit the Herman Low Vision

Aids Clinic, one of the foremost centers for low vision in the entire Southwest. The Herman Clinic had recently acquired the first closed-circuit television read/write system in the state, and the primary reason for my trip was to check out this equipment to see if it could benefit me. That visit introduced me to the machine that would change my life: the Visualtek Read/Write System.

The Visualtek Read/Write System was the very first of the closed-circuit television systems to feature a zoom-lens camera projecting a brilliant image on the TV screen. For someone like me, the implications of this new device were enormous. The system had the ability to dramatically change how I would perform my job, especially paperwork. This contraption looked like nothing I had ever seen. By placing material under the camera's lens, you could see the magnified image on the TV. Because the surface on which reading materials rested could be moved easily, it was possible to move the printed material from left to right and to move the page upward or downward. The availability of this device would mean I could read print of any size and could prepare written materials using the device. Using the device effectively would take some practice, but it would make a huge difference to me.

Mine was the first such device purchased by the Texas State Commission for the Blind. The time at which this machine became available was astounding. How could anyone observe the timing of this event and not see it for what it was—the Lord's timing, the Lord's plan unfolding?

For years I had followed a path, scarcely able to find my way and even less capable of seeing what lay in the distance. All the while, I had believed the Lord would bridge any chasm I could not span on my own. For 25 years I had been preparing for a successful career, and just when I needed a device that would allow me to put all that knowledge to full use, the device suddenly became available to me. Armed with the knowledge that this machine would be provided at no charge to me if I were hired by the planning commission, I was ready for my interview. Gail's mother drove me to the interview because Gail was teaching. I didn't own a suit because I couldn't find one with a 46 long coat and 36 long trousers, but I did put together the sportiest ensemble I could get my hands on. I was ready.

Everything I'd asserted about myself was on the line.

Despite the significance of the moment and occasional spot checks to be sure I had it together, I remained confident. There was no choice—confidence was what had gotten me through undergraduate and postgraduate school. Our plan had been to do everything we could, and leave the rest in the Lord's hands. The interview went exceedingly well; Mr. Crawford even complimented my choice of clothing, commenting that he liked sharp dressers. We had a very pleasant meeting in which Mr. Crawford asked all the right questions, and I had all the right answers. He then hired me on the spot.

I learned that my salary would be paid—at least during the first year— from a program designed to stimulate employment of disabled persons filling certain types of jobs. Urban planning was one of the eligible jobs, and I had the right credentials. The timing couldn't have been better. God's planning was evident.

I would be earning more than any figure reported by my classmates. Plus, I was director of planning for a regional planning commission. I was walking on air! I honestly don't know if my connections, or the fact that my first year's salary was covered, had an impact on the final decision to hire me. I know I was the right candidate, and hoped that was the real reason Mr. Crawford hired me. Regardless, I would work hard to show everyone I deserved the position.

When I returned to the car and told Mrs. Jones the good news, she was as thrilled as I was. She commented that she had been praying for me all the while, and I assured her that I already knew that. We hurried home to share the wonderful news with Gail, and celebrated our good fortune by enjoying a celebratory dinner of Tex-Mex. When I phoned my parents to let them know what had happened, I was especially excited and anxious to tell my father, whose approval still meant the world to me. I wanted to hear the response of the person who had always told me I could do anything. He could scarcely believe the salary: $10,800 (about $65,000 in 2016 dollars)

. . .

On October 11, 1971, I started my new career. My first assignment was to write a procedures manual for the committee I would be leading, the Government Applications Review Committee. I was handed a stack of manuals prepared by other regional planning commissions to use as a model.

As I began reading with what I called my cyclops glasses—they had a huge piece of magnifying glass in the left side and a dummy glass in the right—I felt an unexpected sense of insecurity. Certainly, I had always been self-conscious about having to bury my face in the page to read. I hated being so miserably slow. The knowledge that someone else—anyone else—could do the same work in a fraction of the time bothered me a great deal. Even though I assured myself that not just anyone would have my knowledge of planning, it still gnawed at me.

To add to my angst, I was not the least bit keen on the reporting structure. I was told to work with Karen Ann, Ernie's secretary, to produce the document. Karen Ann was the go-between and would tell me what "Ernie said." It soon became obvious that I only received the feedback that suited Karen Ann's purposes. She had found a way to manipulate her boss. The notion of working through an intermediary didn't set well with me, and I have never worked for someone who engaged in this type of office politics. The whole arrangement added to the insecurity I was feeling at the time.

After a couple of months, the Texas Municipal League invited members of the planning commission's staff to speak at one of their events. I showed up wearing a new suit that my parents had just given me. The pants had been altered unmercifully, but I looked great so long as I kept the coat on to hide the new location of the pockets.

I was on my own when I gave my presentation, and it was extremely well received. Ernie was pleased, and quick to praise me. I received compliments from Jim Brown, the City Manager of Midland, and ended up riding home with him and the Midland delegation. I felt like this was a turning point.

In the months that followed, I had other opportunities to speak, and these opportunities showcased my knowledge and presentation skills. This enhanced my image with public officials, including those on the commission's board of directors. Soon, I gained a reputation for knowing the answer to any statistical question by memory. Before long, it became a point of conversation that I could address a group for a half hour on a highly technical subject without referring to notes. Finally, the skills I had learned out of necessity were helping me turn a potential disadvantage into a strong advantage.

I felt secure in the reputation I enjoyed throughout the region and more confident about my standing with Ernie. However, Karen Ann continued to guard the door to Ernie's office and pass on ultimatums with the prefix, "Ernie said."

Even so, my struggle to be as productive as possible on a daily basis was frustrated by the delay in getting my Visualtek Read/Write System. One of the top executives with the State Commission was trying to back out of purchasing the equipment because he thought I should pay for it out of my own pocket, despite the fact that they had already committed to provide it at no cost. He did this even though the machine had been promised as a condition of my employment. This dragged on for months while I struggled to get by with just my cyclops glasses.

Finally, after waiting for five months, the viewer arrived on leap year day in 1972. Bill Smith, the planning commission's new assistant executive director, helped me assemble the machine. I quickly realized that the equipment had much more potential than I had imagined. After reading a lengthy paragraph using the viewer, I suddenly realized that I hadn't a clue as to what it said. How could this be? I had developed what might be termed an audiographic memory by the time I finished graduate school. Audiographic memory is similar to photographic memory, except that instead of a photograph in my head, I had a recording. It was almost as though I possessed a playback button.

Then it hit me: I had spent nearly 26 years learning how to retain, process, and use what I heard. The pace was so much slower here: 60–70 words per minute versus 175 to 200 spoken words per minute. The very different rate of gathering information was problematic, but the real challenge was the process of using the viewer. The material had to be moved along in just the right manner to expose the next fragment of the line at the right time. The effect of reading this way was to produce a gently moving stream of print similar to a tickertape or a moving stock display. Returning from the end of one line to the beginning of the next proved particularly awkward. Mastering the technique was like learning to rub your stomach while patting your head.

Within a day or two, I was fairly comfortable with the new device. While I still read slowly, I could now read anything—no matter how small the print. I could also now proofread my drafts, whether handwritten or typed. Curiously, I found myself beginning to learn to spell much better by seeing the actual letters used to form the word.

Pretty soon, I was using the viewer for all my work, and the scope of my responsibilities was expanding rapidly as a result. In addition to my work with the Government Applications Review Committee, I supervised a regional housing study and wrote a report detailing its findings. I also directed work on, and helped write, a regional data book.

Work on the regional data book was nearing completion in July of 1973 when I was approached by the City of Midland about becoming its senior city planner. The city was eager to upgrade and expand its planning department, and adding me to the staff was to be the first step. I was being offered an opportunity to play a significant role in shaping the city's future.

Still unsure of my standing with Ernie and thrilled at being asked, I jumped at the chance.

As I went in to see Ernie to tell him of my plans, I didn't know how I should feel.

Would Ernie think me less than loyal and less than appreciative for the opportunity he had given me? In the final analysis, the opportunity to work for Midland's city manager was no decision at all: they had sought me out and it was time to move on. Ernie was gracious and supportive. He pointed out that accepting the position with the City of Midland would allow me to broaden the scope of my experience while working in the city where I lived.

CHAPTER 13

THE ABYSS

While I had a vague idea that Midland was on the verge of awakening from its 15-year slumber, I had no idea that it would soon become one of the fastest growing cities in the United States.

Just two months would pass before the Arab oil embargo would be imposed, and Midland, the administrative hub for 20 percent of the nation's petroleum, would benefit in a big way. The "Tall City," as it had come to be known during the previous boom because of its impressive skyline, was about to become even taller.

Gail and I had been casually looking at houses when we finally found one. I had done enough research to know that houses were dirt cheap in Midland. We were able to buy a three-bedroom brick home with a two-car garage for $13,800. This amounted to less than $10 per square foot. By contrast, new construction was costing $35 to $40 per square foot. A house comparable to ours but located in Dallas, Austin, or Fort Worth would have cost several times what we paid. Given the growth Midland was about to experience, we knew our new home would also be a great investment.

We completely redid the house's interior, painting whenever I wasn't attending school—mostly at night and on weekends. The University of Texas had just opened a branch in nearby Odessa: The University of Texas of the Permian Basin (UTPB). Because the school lacked a doctoral program, I decided to earn a second master's.

For most people, earning two college degrees would have been enough, but not for me. I was addicted to learning—like my motorbike, learning represented freedom. As soon as the school opened in the summer of 1973, I checked it out.

The idea of only working from 8 a.m. to 5 p.m. five days a week was just not in my DNA; I needed more. When I began checking into the new school, I was still at the planning commission, and subconsciously, always had a feeling of uncertainty about what might happen. For me, it was more about doing what I had always done—taking advantage of every opportunity to improve myself and to increase the likelihood that others would recognize me for my skills instead of my disability. Because I was legally blind, there was always that underlying feeling of having to prove myself. Based on my experiences up to that time, a lack of sight seemed to indicate to some people that I should know my place and stay in it. After a lifetime of struggling to achieve academic success, I now had two powerful new tools to make learning easier: a cassette recorder and a magnifier/reader. Both of these tools made it so much easier for me to learn.

I ended up enrolling in three classes, and I listened to my textbooks as we painted the house. Now and again, Gail would come by and point out a spot I had missed—probably a combination of my poor eyesight and focusing more on listening than painting.

The dramatic population growth I foresaw materialized with shocking speed. My own expectations would be exceeded, and I began to develop a strategy for meeting the challenges ahead.

The first thing I did was to create a 110-page "Similar Cities" study of 13 communities comparable to Midland. The study provided some insights about the track record of various public policies and expenditures.

Soon after I conceived the idea of the Similar Cities study, I was contacted by the Texas Department of Community Affairs, with whom I had collaborated before; they wanted us to participate in a project with the LBJ School of Public Affairs at the University of Texas at Austin. I was recommended to spearhead the project for Midland.

George Wolf, my boss, and I attended the first meeting in Austin, and laughed about the striking parallels between this project and our own Similar Cities Study. One of the most gratifying features of our project with the LBJ School was the level of support given it by Jim Brown, Midland City Manager. He made the 700-mile round trip to Austin with us several times just to participate in this project; his support meant a lot to me.

As the summer approached, I worked hard to complete the city's overall work program—a kind of "planners' plan." The program established goals and objectives for each of the next three years, a challenge I embraced. George afforded me a great deal of latitude, which helped me be effective. His academic background had not included urban planning, although he did have a degree in architecture. Like his boss, the city manager, George was deferential towards me and followed my lead when it came to issues of urban planning. His expertise was centered on zoning issues, an area that I didn't have as much knowledge in—we were a good team, balancing each other. Unlike the negative experiences I encountered when I was attending school, almost all of my colleagues were supportive and didn't treat me differently.

Soon, I was charged with assembling a team of interns to work on a research project.

To be effective, I believed a planning department should know as much as possible about the city it served. Just about everything that could be recorded, measured, or evaluated would become part of our study. During the course of the study, the opportunity for creative thinking endeared me to city planning, even as I was simultaneously studying to either teach psychology at night or perhaps become a professional counselor. The head of the counseling program at UTPB encouraged me to change careers and become a counselor, just as the head of A&M's counseling program had done when I was there. Although I never made the change, my career path eventually morphed into a type of counseling. I never lost my desire to encourage and instruct anyone who might benefit from my advice.

For as long as I can remember, my mind has been an idea factory. While it is hard to be certain where my creativity originates, I can't help but think that it is the result of having to compensate for my poor eyesight. I have a hypothesis that persons with limited eyesight are more likely to have vivid imaginations than the general population.

Everyday life for someone visually impaired consists of dozens, perhaps hundreds, of situations calling for conjecture. Every time you encounter someone in the hall, on the sidewalk, or entering a room, you are forced to gather data and form a hypothesis as to that person's identity. Every step, every voice, every glimpse or sound causes your mind to speculate. Not only has this phenomenon honed my intellectual skills, it has shaped my soul.

It was the confluence of two forces during my years as senior city planner that caused me to form my "hypothesis about hypotheses." My job allowed me to be as creative as I wanted, and the postgraduate studies I had resumed were focused on educational psychology and counseling, my secondary field of study at A&M.

I realized more than ever that my greatest frailty—poor eyesight—had fostered my greatest faculty, creative thinking. I really enjoyed coming up with new ideas for solving problems or just enriching the lives of others.

This characteristic is a symptom of a broader intellectual condition. Psychologists refer to this trait or syndrome as psychological gradient, and it is characterized by the need to be mentally active at a high level most of the time. The idea behind the concept can be visualized by picturing someone walking uphill. This trait itself proved part of an even larger characteristic—I was (and still am) an incurable "achieveaholic." Fortunately, I was not a "jobaholic." The scope of my interests was much broader than just my job; however, the job always got my very best effort. My early years as a planner provided exceptional opportunities for psychological gradient and for worthwhile and enjoyable work. After attending night school at UTPB for three or four semesters, I learned that I had more than the minimum number of graduate hours for a Ph.D. in the University of Texas system, in at least some areas of study.

About the same time, I learned that the University of Texas at Arlington (UTA) offered a Ph.D. in urban administration. I checked into the program requirements to see if I might participate with a minimum residency requirement. It looked like I could complete the program by attending a five-week summer session, writing a dissertation, and passing oral examinations. Earning this degree seemed a logical step toward becoming a city manager.

Since Gail was teaching school, she had the summer off and could accompany me. Having her with me meant, among many other things, she could be my reader.

Before presenting my plans to the city manager, I was able to get a commitment from the curriculum counselor at UTA to take the required nine Ph.D.-level hours during a single "short semester" lasting only five weeks. Believing I would never get a better opportunity than this, I asked the city manager if I might be allowed the time off. I agreed to his request that I remain with the City of Midland at least two years, preferably three, in exchange for the time off.

On our way to Arlington, we stopped off at Mineral Wells and borrowed a card table from my parents to use as a makeshift desk. Once I placed my viewer on it, it looked like a beast of burden. As small as this work surface was, it was all that there was room for in the tiny one-bedroom apartment we rented.

Although we were careful not to run up our expenses, I told Gail that this was the way to attend graduate school: driving a late model Buick and earning combined salaries of $29,000 a year (about $100,000 in today's dollars). Just before we left town, Gail had been promoted to Coordinator of Early Childhood Development and English Language for the Midland Independent School District (MISD). At 27, she was the youngest person ever to be promoted to an equivalent position with MISD.

My agreement with the city manager provided that I would continue to draw my full salary during my absence. This meant, we could afford to eat out frequently and have fun on the weekends to the extent that my study schedule would permit. Even so, I grew weary of that small dark apartment and even more weary of having to concentrate on listening or reading nearly every waking moment I spent there. The pace was a rigorous one, even for someone like me, who thrived on it. A course load of six hours in six weeks was considered a full academic load—I was managing nine hours in five weeks.

With Gail reading and/or recording most of the material, I did well and earned excellent grades. After I had successfully completed my coursework, my counselor told me that he was no longer so sure that I wouldn't be needing to complete some more courses—on campus. I felt misled and very frustrated. The expectation that I could satisfy the residency requirement had been a big part of my decision to enroll. I had never considered that I might have to return later.

When I explained that the requirement for any additional on-campus courses would effectively destroy my hopes of completing the degree, an alternative was offered—any additional courses could be completed at the Odessa campus, UTPB.

Once we returned to Midland and settled back in, I received word that there was another course I would have to take, but that I could take it at the Odessa campus. When fall came, I uncharacteristically registered for one course. This was like driving 20 miles to the supermarket just to buy one loaf of bread. It was not a challenge; it was a nuisance. Long after I had abandoned all hope that that semester would someday end, it finally did. This exacerbated my sense of the long, drawn out, and, even worse, nebulous time frame for completing my Ph.D.

By now, I had very little comfort that I could count on any particular timetable. Moreover, the more I thought about writing a dissertation, the more apparent it became to me that not a single professor in the Department of Urban Administration had ever worked for a city in any capacity. While I had attended class at UTA, I found myself instructing both professors and classmates in urban administration. I disagreed with the department's policies on other issues, so I began to consider another approach to becoming a city manager. I dropped out of the Ph.D. program and decided to earn an MBA instead.

There were certainly other factors influencing my decision. Gail and I were expecting our first child. Things at the office were not the same. Jim Brown was struggling to perform his duties as city manager while battling recently diagnosed cancer, and pressure mounted from the city council for strong leadership from the planning department.

Strong leadership meant a strong department head. This created a sticky internal situation, and the decision was made to hire an outsider for the position. An effort was made to appease George Wolf, who had long held the position, by selecting a man significantly older than I was. Dr. Robert Giles, a Ph.D. in government, was chosen in part to accommodate my desire for an academically gifted supervisor. Unfortunately, Dr. Giles' academic background was of little use, because he had no practical experience in city planning.

While Dr. Giles was gracious to me, it quickly became apparent that he could not provide the level of technical guidance needed, and was unable to get along with other key officials. I thought he would either be terminated or his ineptness simply tolerated. If it was the latter, I knew I would be frustrated and have no way of advancing in the department. Getting my MBA was even more critical.

Before solidifying my plans to transition to an MBA, I contacted Dr. Nini, the head of the School of Management at UTPB, and asked him how many hours I would need to complete the requirements for an MBA, as well as whether he would grant me special permission to take that number of hours during a single semester at night. Dr. Nini agreed to let me take the seven courses during a single semester. He justified it based on my track record: I had been successful at three different universities' graduate programs, and I should know better than anyone else my capabilities.

In order to take all these courses in such limited time, I took as many as I could self-paced. For me, attacking this challenge was like everything else in life. I figured some innovation and an enormous commitment to hard work would do the trick. At this point in my life, I had tons of energy and drive. After so many years of struggling through college, I now had the right tools, including the right equipment. I was confident the experience would be much smoother, so I decided to use every brief lull in my classroom courses between exams and papers to study for self-paced courses.

My plan was to complete two self-paced courses by the third month, thereby reducing my course load to five—even if it meant settling for a couple of Bs. I would use my vacation days to study for each test in the self-paced courses. Typically, these tests would cover from one-third to one-half of the material in a course. By listening to the materials on tape, I could read everything at least once in that amount of time.

Farrell Jean Washam, a friend, did almost all of my reading, keeping me in a seemingly endless stream of tapes. Staying home with her young son (not to mention expecting her second child), she was able to accommodate me— plus, she worked cheap. Farrell did an amazing job and delivered her baby just as I was wrapping up my last semester. On graduation day, I left mailing instructions for my diploma, and went fishing instead.

The timing of my graduation seemed perfect. Within a matter of days, the planning director was, in fact, dismissed, leaving an opening for me.

I didn't lose any time in letting Mr. Brown know I was interested. Then I waited. Each day I hoped there would be an announcement; each day there was silence. Finally, someone from the City of Amarillo's planning office was hired.

I was deeply disappointed and frustrated but unfortunately not surprised; I was pretty sure the mayor objected to me personally. In fact, he told me directly that he didn't like planning. This statement took me aback. The mayor believed planning, including land use and zoning, to be similar to communism. He told me I had angered the city council by stating that Midland's population had actually gone down even though the number of electric meters had increased. Only after the 1980 census figures were released did he realize that a reduction in family size had more than offset the net gains in occupied structures. But the mayor's biggest reason for not wanting me promoted was a misstep I had made within weeks of joining the city. A half-baked proposal came before the Planning & Zoning Commission to locate a major regional mall on a street that couldn't accommodate the traffic. In my zeal to nix the plan, I had suggested that Midland couldn't support a regional mall. That position sounded defeatist and reflected my lack of personal experience. While I believed I had the full confidence of the city manager, who had spent a great deal of time getting to know me and my work, the mayor had far fewer facts on which to evaluate me. Politics once again tied the hands of the city manager. Certainly, there was no one who wanted this position more than I did—and, in my opinion, no one who was better qualified.

As it turned out, my opinion had been wrong. The new head, Richard Hennessy, turned out to be smart, had great experience, and held an undergraduate degree in civil engineering. Richard had a better understanding of the physical aspects of city planning than I did. I very quickly recognized his intellect and leadership, and quickly conveyed this to my staff, all of whom were very loyal to me. I saw him as an exceptionally clear thinker and good to work for. Perhaps most important, he was someone from whom I could learn a great deal. Sometimes individuals with disabilities get passed over for a promotion for reasons that have nothing to do with being disabled—there is simply a more qualified candidate. Once I got my ego in check, I realized that about Richard.

...

Only two weeks after Richard arrived to assume his duties as head of the planning department, Gail gave birth to our daughter, Beth Ann. I was never prouder. Life was good.

Once Beth Ann was home, the wonder of having her was even greater. At that moment, I realized that it is impossible to describe what I felt as a parent to someone without children. I believed my joy and appreciation of my daughter was particularly keen because of my years of caring for Janie. I already knew how to love someone who was helpless, and I knew all too well how to savor the gift of a healthy child.

Eventually, Gail stayed home to care for Beth Ann. She taught a course at Midland College, and I stepped up my teaching load as an adjunct professor there. I had begun teaching in 1972, before the college even had a permanent home.

As one might expect, teaching college without being able to see a word of the text or notes presented some challenges. While this could have been intimidating, instead it was pure joy. The Midland Recording Library for the Blind & Physically Handicapped recorded the textbook for me and even read the essays my students wrote. From my perspective, this was an ideal way for me to grade exams, because the name associated with each exam was not disclosed until after I had determined a grade. Rather than strictly lecturing, I announced each major topic and randomly called on students to discuss the material. Using a steady stream of humor, I managed to pull each student into the action, and stood by to flesh out the details. Favorable feedback from my students led to an opportunity to teach government for several years. I took a hiatus from teaching at Midland College to focus on the seven graduate courses I had undertaken during the spring semester of 1976. Then, in 1977, with my second master's degree under my belt, I was contacted by UTPB to teach Public Administration, one night a week for a semester. To earn additional income, I also painted houses and mowed lawns in our neighborhood. As usual, Gail and I did whatever it took to make ends meet. And as I mentioned earlier, I was never one to stop at 9-to-5.

Even so, the odd jobs barely generated enough income to offset our giving to our church, now that Gail wasn't working full-time and we had a child to support. At the beginning of our marriage, Gail and I had decided we were going to tithe, and we continued that commitment. Our view has been that tithing forces you to make a decision to live on the periphery of your faith or to commit to it. We chose to commit.

During this period, I continued to look for new ways to earn more money while enhancing my personal and professional development. One of the first things I did was to study for the exams to become a member of the American Institute of Certified Planners (AICP)—the highest designation available to urban and regional planners. To take the test, I had to grab a plane to Dallas and spend a morning being grilled by a committee made up of folks who already held the designation. Once the exam was over, I was told I'd hear their decision within the next couple of weeks. During lunch, one of the examiners remarked that it had taken him two tries to pass, and another said he had failed the exam three times before finally being successful. My heart sank, but two weeks later, I heard from the AICP: I had passed!

I was elected to the board of directors of the City Planners Association of Texas. My position entailed writing and editing the association's newsletter. This new role incentivized me to improve my grammar and writing skills by finding a tutor to help me. I contacted a retired high school English teacher, and she was willing to help. What followed amazed me. Within seven weeks of instruction, one night per week, I saw an astonishing level of improvement and an increased sense of confidence in my writing. What surprised me most was the speed and ease with which I began to master the knowledge that had so long seemed beyond my reach. For the next four years, my work as editor on the newsletter benefited from my improved skills. Developing my writing skills had been a long-term goal and priority. After all, the major goal I had established for myself as a high school senior was "to become the sculptor of elegant and compelling thoughts both as a writer and a speaker."

. . .

By early 1980, the outlook for oil investments was deteriorating, as was the outlook for my advancement at City Hall. We were expecting our second child in March, and for the first time in my life, I was out of ideas for moving forward.

On Saturday, February 16, as I lay in bed, and having no structure for the day, I began to feel down and out. Saturdays had always been my least favorite day because they afforded me free time; well, sort of free time. During the lawn mowing season, late March to mid-October, my enormous lawn beckoned and that of others as well. By contrast, this mid-February day offered no such game plan for the day—no structure. I loved my family and the time we spent together, but I couldn't involve myself in physical activities that other fathers did get to enjoy on the weekends. Weekends reminded me that I didn't have the same structure at home that I did while at the office. As I lay there, I reflected upon the remarks of the speaker we had heard the night before at our church's Sweetheart Banquet. One-by-one he asked each of us privately to answer a question. Each time, after hearing him describe how he thought Christ would have answered the question or would have responded,

I compared my response and noted to myself that I was scoring a perfect 10—not once or twice but every time. One could be excused for thinking this would have pleased me. Not at all. Why, I wondered, after nearly decades of working so hard and with such Herculean energy and thoughtfulness, did I find myself in a dead-end job that could define the remaining 30–40 years of my career? Wasn't there someone out there who knew I had invested at least the equivalent of eight full-time years to earn three college degrees and a fourth in all but name? Did it not matter that I had worked from 70 to more than 100 hours per week throughout my career? What is more, for nearly a decade, Gail and I had given until it hurt of time and resources to support the Lord's work. I remember the date precisely because it was such a traumatic event—I had never experienced this kind of depression before.

My mind turned to a role model I had known at First Baptist Church College Station, who was also the head of one of the most important departments at Texas A&M. His name was Dr. Tony Sorenson, but he introduced himself to me as Tony Sorenson. He sang in the choir (including occasional solos), and helped start mission churches at First Baptist, where his wife, Tommie, was church pianist. This couple served for years as Mom and Pop Sorenson. Observing them parent their own kids and act as surrogate parents for untold other youngsters caused me to see them as the most ideal role models I had encountered. Clearly, Dr. Sorenson was someone I wanted to emulate. At this juncture, comparing the career path I envisioned for myself to his saddened me further. Exacerbating my feelings, I felt and continued to have an awful premonition that something bad was going to happen to my role model. Four weeks later, Dr. Malcom Bane, pastor of First Baptist College Station, came to our church to lead a revival. That's when I found out that Dr. Sorenson had suddenly dropped dead of a heart attack just four days after my premonition. He was only 55. I have no idea why I had experienced the premonition, nor am I sure why exactly, but his death had a profound impact on me. After all, I hadn't seen or spoken to any of the Sorensons since graduating and moving to West Texas some nine years earlier. Perhaps the senselessness of it all reinforced my feeling that no one was in control. Why would this person who was an authority on animal science, who jogged six days every week, whose father had lived to age 86…die so young? Perhaps more disturbing to me, why would someone whose every minute had been devoted to serving the

Lord and living an exemplary life—just die? This event reinforced my feeling of hopelessness that I had begun to experience for the first time. These feelings infected my entire life, but especially my marriage. For the next eight months, I suffered constantly, obsessed by thoughts of regret and hopelessness. Everything I had loved I was now estranged from—especially family work and church.

The beginning of my ascent out of this emotional hell came when Gail, our seven-month-old daughter Becky, and I traveled to Ruidoso, New Mexico, for two weeks. Beth Ann, four at the time, stayed with Gail's mom. We went there on the recommendation of friends to see a doctor about my eyes. The doctor failed to benefit me, but the time away did.

I realized that our marriage could work, and that I could be happy. Gail shared a cassette with me about a book titled *Men in Midlife Crisis* by Jim Conway. Learning that most men—especially overachievers like me—go through such a time helped a lot. Conway described the characteristics, and they fit me perfectly: All of a sudden, everything you have loved, especially God and your spouse, become estranged. Many men daydream about jumping in a car and just driving. Needless to say, I didn't bother to fantasize about that, since it was out of the question. I also learned that many men, when going through this misery, change jobs and/or spouses. My perception that I was stuck in a dead-end job for life was a major cause for my downward spiral in the first place. And the idea of changing spouses was repugnant to me. Gail had been the treasure of my life and would be again. The tremendous drive that had always benefited me so much had turned against me. I was confronted with a situation, for the first time in my life, when trying harder seemed useless. Fortunately, just realizing that many, many men face this—and that there is light at the other end of the tunnel—provided hope. I felt reinvigorated, realizing that Gail and the girls could provide so much pleasure and joy in my life. Throughout my ordeal, there was one and only one hero, and that person was Gail. The truth is that it had been just as much an ordeal for her as for me. While I never abused her physically or verbally, she nonetheless endured rejection, but had enough wisdom and strength of character to uncover the problem and reveal it to me. What we rediscovered after this dark episode has been more special than anything we had before it.

My personal life having been restored, I turned my efforts to work, producing a major update to the city's Comprehensive Plan. My plan began to gain traction, and a consultant was hired to assist us.

My work was once again fulfilling, and I was back to my old self. Not only did the consultant provide excellent direction to my work and those supporting me, but so did my boss, Richard Hennessy. As a result, in March of 1981 I had the privilege of giving the first major presentation of our work to the city's Planning & Zoning Commission. Strong, yet ambivalent feelings washed over me during that meeting: I would be leaving after almost eight years. Richard introduced me by announcing that I had been offered, and had accepted, a position with The First National Bank of Midland, an institution that for nearly a century had been the most prestigious corporate entity in Midland.

Near the end of my presentation, word reached us that President Reagan had been shot. When I learned he would be okay, it seemed a fitting metaphor for the way things had turned out for me. While I was overjoyed at being able to move on from a career that presented very little hope of advancement, I was thankful that I never perceived the slightest discrimination related to my visual impairment. On the contrary, I believe people such as Jim Brown and Richard Hennessy never swerved in their confidence in my intellect and work ethic. It is difficult to imagine how I could have parted with more positive feelings toward and from my fellow employees.

CHAPTER 14

PRIDE AND PAIN

Gail had taken a selfless pride in my new job. I will never forget her words when I telephoned to say that I had received a job offer from the bank: "I am so proud for you." It is so critical to have a partner in life, and I found mine in Gail.

Instead of having to disassemble and lug my viewer to my new office, the bank had already arranged for me to get a smaller and vastly improved model. Doug Henson, my new boss, instructed me to get the viewer I thought would be best. He arranged to have the old viewer delivered to my home. This generosity by the bank let me know that I was valued; the senior management had embraced my disability and pledged to provide anything I needed to deal with it effectively. After having worked for two government organizations for the first 10 years of my career, I found it refreshing that my employer was so supportive they would provide me with tools that exceeded the standards of basic utility.

The new machine was much better than the old one. Moreover, it fit nicely above the opening in the gorgeous teakwood credenza situated behind a matching desk—what you would expect at a bank but quite different from what I was used to! I no longer occupied a plain veneer table, largely consumed by a huge, two-piece contraption strung together with various cables and wires. No longer was I shoved into one corner of a would-be drafting room hosting four other individuals. For the first time in my professional career, I had my own office.

As I leaned back in my chair, I looked across Wall Avenue (yes, the street was really named Wall Avenue) at another skyscraper and thought about how far I had come. Doug Henson came into my office carrying a solid gold eagle lapel pin—the symbol of my new status as an officer of the bank. With considerable pride, I attached it to my new suit.

He explained that one of my official responsibilities as an officer would be to take customers and prospective customers to lunch at least three times per week in the Bank's executive dining room located on the 24th floor. He went on to explain that it was all entirely free to bank officers. The contrast between city hall and the bank couldn't have been greater.

"This place is unbelievable," I remarked. While all this was a bonus that came with being a bank officer, it was much more than a perk. The dining room was a way to court potential customers and demonstrate the bank's financial strength and presence. The bank wanted the ability to host customers on its own turf.

I had been hired as Assistant Vice President of Marketing Research. In this role, I would be editor of the bank's monthly newsletter, *The Economic Activity Report*. I would also assist the bank in formulating plans, conducting special studies, formulating marketing strategies, advising on real estate and other urban planning matters, counseling customers and prospects about the local business climate, and making presentations to every civic organization in town, as well as on radio and television. I felt as if I had died and gone to heaven!

The pace I inherited was suited to the times. In 1981, Midland's population was growing at least twice as fast as other booming cities in the country. Apartment complexes and office buildings boasted occupancy rates averaging in excess of 97 percent. People were living in travel trailers, motor homes, and even tents. Over the previous eight years, the price of oil had risen 1,100 percent. Excess was all the rage, including at the bank.

A full-scale boom was underway, and I was thrust into its center. The First National Bank of Midland was the unquestioned corporate leader of Midland, and I, or so it seemed, might help shape its strategy. During my first week with the bank, a news conference was called and it was announced that the bank had acquired eight acres of additional land surrounding its original grounds and would be constructing twin 40-story towers. That news brought my euphoria to a screeching halt.

I was convinced it was a mistake to announce, let alone undertake, such a massive project. I knew that a population increase of roughly 28,000 would be required to create enough office demand to fill these two huge structures, something that would take several years—even at the current explosive growth rate. I also knew that adequate research had not been conducted in support of this decision because I had been paid a visit by a representative of the consulting firm conducting the feasibility study for this project, while I was still at city hall.

During that meeting, it quickly became obvious the consultant didn't know how to conduct such a study and didn't know much about Midland. Somebody at a very high level was shooting from the hip, and that made me nervous.

The next red flag appeared when I completed my review and synopsis of the consultant's report—after the bank had already announced its plans. At the end of my review, I told the bank's CFO the plan made no provision for a downturn in the petroleum industry—ever. And we all know I knew enough about economics to realize that extreme circumstances always get adjusted in the opposite direction.

Together we developed what the CFO called the "jump now" plan. The bank's stock was selling for more than $90 per share if you could find anyone willing to sell, because public sentiment toward the institution was at an all-time high. We agreed the bank should issue a $100 million stock offering and use the money to recapitalize the bank as a hedge against any future reversals.

Very early on, I realized that some consulting firms simply prostitute themselves for big bucks, and the one that had completed this study exemplified that culture. They were all too happy to produce a plan showing nothing but blue skies forever and a report recommending two enormous towers. The bank's president agreed with their findings. Actually, they merely wrote down what the president wanted them to say and pocketed the money.

As a professional planner, and employee of the bank, I found this unacceptable—and frightening. I made it a personal goal of entering the president's inner circle so I could have a stronger impact on the decisions being made.

Before long, my efforts paid off—the president was passing along invitations to speak at various functions, giving me the opportunity to showcase my talents. Those efforts led to me being charged with estimating the total demand for additional rigs in the Permian Basin for the balance of the year and examining the long-term potential for exploration in the region. I hoped to be able to convince the powers that be that the current rate of growth was not sustainable, and we were headed for a market that was oversupplied. Unfortunately, because I didn't call the shots, the bank's leadership did not heed my warnings and continued to overextend.

...

As my work on the project was concluding in early June, I learned that Janie was in the hospital, critically ill.

After 31 long years of hanging on, it was clear that the end was near for my beloved sister. My parents, in their characteristic manner, took turns sleeping and caring for her. This went on day and night for more than a week. They found a spot in the hospital's parking lot for the little motor home they had bought four years earlier to transport Janie. This provided a small sanctuary from which they could operate. As always, my limited sight and inability to drive meant there was no practical way for me to make a quick overnight trip to Mineral Wells to relieve my parents. Fortunately, when my brother Jimmy came to relieve our parents so they could get some rest, Janie passed. I am forever grateful that he was holding her hand when she died. This was such a blessing to our parents—and to me.

Because I had earned no leave of any kind on my new job and couldn't make a quick trip, I made the tough decision to wait until after Janie died to go home, with the intent to be there to comfort my parents. I left as quickly as possible that Tuesday morning, June 9, 1981. When the end came, Doug urged me not to return until the following week.

Just as Janie had produced great emotions in those of us who loved and cared for her during her lifetime, her death was no different. As I expected, her death was especially hard on my father. Certainly, he shared our sense of relief that her suffering had finally ended. Still, he grieved bitterly as one having nurtured an infant for three decades only to lose that child.

High-sounding theology about a loving God goes down hard for a parent at such a time—it was easier for me. My daughters were alive and healthy, and I had known a loving father—a sort of role model for God. Daddy had not been so fortunate—not by a long shot. It had always been a curious privilege for me to hear the thoughts of someone so brilliant and so unencumbered by convention as he contemplated such matters.

As I sat through the funeral service, I pondered the possibility that this idea of God is no more than an outgrowth of a common childhood experience. Perhaps it is realizing that someone cares for you and somehow knows what you have been doing even when that person is nowhere in sight. Since junior high, I had often thought religion might be merely a device for promoting social order. Maybe it is just a defense mechanism for reconciling the irreconcilable, a way of grasping allegory when, in fact, good actually fails to triumph over evil. Just maybe, I thought, we are Christians for the same reasons that Muslims are Muslims and Buddhists are Buddhists. Perhaps we believe what we were brought up to believe. Surely, I thought, there is a measure of truth in all these thoughts. Even so, I knew that I believed Jesus Christ was who He said He was.

From my study of philosophy, I knew Jesus Christ was the only major religious figure in history to claim He was God. From my study of the Bible, I knew Jesus possessed a personhood like no other. He was worthy of the honor bestowed upon Him by history—that human experience on earth should be measured using a system of time synchronized to His life and death. I was especially pleased when the preacher read from John 14: "In my Father's house there are many mansions: if it were not so, I would have told you. I go to prepare a place for you." I felt that Jesus would no sooner have whitewashed something bad than would my own father.

This scripture gave me considerable comfort. I believed that Janie was finally liberated and finally whole. Also, I believed that her life and even her illness had served a very great purpose in my life. Perhaps even more than my father, Janie had affected my response to life. Everything that I had accomplished and every achievement that lay ahead could be traced to my feelings about her. She had helped me answer the most important question of all, "What has value in life?" Through Janie, and my parents' attention to her, I learned about loving, caring, nurturing, instructing, and inspiring—all the attributes I value.

Once we moved from the church to the cemetery, and the pallbearers began unloading the casket, Daddy came to me and asked if I would like to get closer to the casket in order to see it better. As I gazed toward the back of the hearse, I could make out, through my tears, the pink blur. Having helped Jimmy and Mary select the casket the night before, I had a clear picture of it in my mind and decided that was close enough.

As I considered what this ordeal was like for others, I was so thankful that my father could take some encouragement from the wonderful things that were taking place in my life. Only two months had lapsed since I had told him about my new position at the bank. I remembered the obvious pleasure in his voice and thought perhaps it had been part of God's plan to ease the awful sting that lay ahead.

The next day I asked Daddy if he would like me to help him dismantle the special chair he had constructed for Janie so many years earlier. Somehow, doing this made her passing official. It was the last painful ceremony that had to be endured, and I was not about to have him go through it alone.

On Friday, I went with Daddy on his service calls. In many ways, it was like old times. But it was mostly an effort to return to business as usual—to get on with life. We spoke of his plans for the business, in its 47th year, and of my plans at the bank.

. . .

When I returned to work, I was thankful for the rapid pace and fulfillment. I managed to complete the study within a couple of weeks. What made this process so exhilarating was my ability to keep an updated record of everything in my mind—without referring to notes.

Virtually every number I encountered was automatically committed to memory; its meaning made it inherently memorable. One of the few benefits of being visually impaired, this gift allowed me to test hypotheses anytime, anywhere. Possessing this aptitude meant that I would be able to present a 30-page report to the management committee without having to read anything. I would use some large wall-mounted exhibits, featuring a print size large enough for me to read while standing in front of them, but frankly, these were for the benefit of the committee. I did not need them.

Finally, the big day came, and I was pleased with my presentation and the committee's response to it. I ended my presentation by making a very specific prediction of drilling rig growth for the final six months of the year.

Perhaps to keep my thoughts away from Janie's death, I focused on another big event in my life. Doug Henson, the very person who brought me to the Bank, announced his resignation. Having been onboard just three or four months, this turn of events could have been unsettling for me—Doug had been a big supporter. However, senior level officers had already commented on me as one of the most gifted young officers at the bank. It helped that I was responsible for producing a monthly report the bank had been publishing for years—an important part of its marketing and outreach.

Doug's departure opened the position of Vice President, Marketing. I was one of two viable candidates. The other, Guy McCrary, had been with the bank longer, and enjoyed a well-deserved reputation as an extremely polished professional. His expertise was in the advertising end of the marketing function. I figured the decision was too close to call. No decision was made for more than a year.

...

As 1981 drew to a close, something terrifying happened to our daughter Becky—something we will never forget. At just 21 months old, she began to bruise very easily, all over her body. Not surprisingly, Gail was the first to notice a nasty bruise near Becky's left eye. After checking over her carefully, Gail rushed her to see our pediatrician to get some answers. With tears in her voice, Gail telephoned me from the doctor's office, and gave me the bad news: "The doctor wants me to take Becky straight to the hospital; something is wrong. He is afraid she may have leukemia."

Soon after they arrived at the hospital, a blood platelet count was ordered to see if her blood was capable of clotting properly. Sure enough, her count was only about one percent of normal. Gail and I were instructed to take turns standing beside her bed holding her arms to prevent her from bumping against anything. Otherwise, she might bleed to death. A refrigerated container of platelets would have to be flown in from Dallas, and this would take several hours.

Once the platelets arrived, Becky was given an I.V. injection in the top of her head; we would have to wait to see if her body assimilated or consumed them. This procedure was performed at about 1 a.m. Gail and I were placed outside the room where Becky was taken. We could hear her screams in response to the pain and frightening circumstances. Gail and I were utterly distraught. The next morning, we were informed that she had already lost about 98 percent of the injected platelets. We were told that this was exactly the effect that would *not* be produced by leukemia. On one hand, this was wonderful news, but we were still faced with a life-threatening disease and had no clue what the real problem was.

Both our family doctor and pediatrician said they had never seen anything like this. They decided to contact a larger urban medical center for advice. The person they reached said he knew exactly what was wrong and what to do about it. It was not leukemia but a rare disorder known as ITP, and to our relief, we learned that the disorder is completely treatable.

Within a few days, we brought Becky home from the hospital. Only a few days after that, we traveled to my parents' house to celebrate Christmas. There we rejoiced over the best Christmas present our family could ever receive: our precious toddler was home from the hospital. She was out of the woods and the prognosis was a full and complete recovery.

Our family's crisis had ended in joy. Many hours had been invested in prayer. While I understood how some intelligent individuals could presume that prayer had nothing to do with the favorable outcome, Gail and I believe the Lord answers prayer.

That year—1981—had been an emotionally charged one. My move to the bank had been a joyous step, not just for me but for our entire family. Janie's death had been a mixture of grief and relief, and Becky's illness created a roller coaster of feelings that started with distress and dread but ended in unspeakable joy.

Little did we know that the three years ahead would be filled with even more anxiety.

CHAPTER 15

TWICE THE HEARTBREAK

In early 1982, I learned that my forecast regarding the number of drilling rigs was strikingly close to actual numbers. While I was at first elated that I had done such a good job, I soon discovered that the inventory of rigs had increased around the country. It was clear to me the bank was on a slippery slope, but it had never been my nature to react to a piece of potentially bad news as though the sky were falling. After all, the bank had been making energy loans for more than 90 years, and the industry literature had not uttered a word about the oncoming tidal wave I believed I had discovered.

While I was waiting to see if my instincts were correct, another unnerving series of events began to unfold. When Beth Ann was 5 years old, Gail told me that she was seeing indications that our daughter's vision was declining. Gail was an authority in early childhood development, but I was still reluctant to accept what she was telling me. Virtually every eye care professional I had seen beginning in junior high had told me that my condition is not hereditary. Gail shared with me that Beth Ann looked at a classmate's paper during an assignment; the teacher informed us that our child was cheating. Gail remarked to me that the idea of Beth Ann cheating made no sense. She was already the top performing student in her class, and had never shown any inclination to cheat at anything. Gail instinctively saw it for what it was: deficient eyesight. I thought Beth Ann might just need glasses, but her eye care professional didn't detect anything particularly out of the ordinary. If I hadn't been told more than once that my condition wasn't hereditary—and that there was no possible way to pass the gene to my heirs—I would have been more concerned.

The following year, Beth Ann's first grade teacher told us she could not see the chalkboard. This new observation started us on a journey that lasted nearly three years and took us to specialists in four cities. The first physician we saw was a local ophthalmologist. He shined a bright light in our daughter's eyes, which produced a stream of tears and caused her to cry. According to Gail, the doctor was abrasive and dismissive of Beth Ann's reaction, and this treatment just exacerbated things. We got no answers from the doctor. The only thing we knew for sure was that we would never return to that physician's office again.

Looking for emotional comfort—as well as an explanation of why Beth Ann was suffering—we turned to our faith, and met with our pastor. He suggested we see a pediatric ophthalmologist in Dallas who had successfully treated his young son's juvenile cataracts. After school was out in June, the three of us—myself, Gail and Beth Ann—made the trip. I had not accompanied Gail and Beth Ann to the first appointment in Midland, and felt it was important to be there this time. More importantly, I wanted to assist Gail in advocating for our daughter. This time, the physician was pleasant enough, but he was unable to identify the problem—or even to confirm our belief that a problem existed. In fact, he assessed her visual acuity at 20/50—according to him, this was not unusual for a child who was 7 years old. Even though we had informed him of my optic nerve atrophy, he insisted that his diagnosis was correct because he subscribed to the view that had been so often shared with me—that optic nerve atrophy is not hereditary.

We were cautiously optimistic when told our daughter's vision might improve with age, and if it did not, she only had a fraction (1/20th) of the impairment I had. Beth Ann was a happy, well-adjusted child who was doing well at school. While I certainly considered myself well-adjusted when I was her age, I didn't perform well in school. I accepted the doctor's findings.

While all of this was going on with Beth Ann, my predictions about the viability of the bank started to come true. My research into past drilling patterns suggested a possible pickup in drilling in August, but this never materialized. Everyone was on edge and distracted, including me.

As second grade drew to a close in 1983, our family's focus returned to Beth Ann's vision problems. Beth Ann was about to turn 8 years old when her teacher informed us that her sight had not improved perceptively, and was clearly inferior to that of her classmates. She had taken a strong interest in Beth Ann and noticed that she was having a difficult time seeing the blackboard compared to her classmates. This was a turning point for me, one where I began to strongly suspect the medical textbooks and the doctors who we trusted with religious devotion were dead wrong. Gail had already reached that conclusion. For the first time, I began to feel a sense of foreboding that something was wrong that might not be correctable. More and more, it was looking like I had poisoned the water for Beth Ann and perhaps even Becky. Searching for practical help, we learned about an optometrist in Odessa who specialized in visual therapy, Dr. Donald Hembree. Dr. Hembree was a pioneer in using a particular type of exercise for the eyes. He discovered that Beth Ann had significant difficulty discerning shades of red—the first useful information we had received since we started our search for answers almost two years earlier. After several months of therapy and exercises produced no measurable improvement, Dr. Hembree was convinced something else was going on. He recommended we see a neurological ophthalmologist at Texas Tech Medical School.

While all of this was going on, Beth Ann's teacher recommended her for the gifted and talented (GT) program when she entered the third grade in the spring of 1984—even though she had trouble seeing. Beth Ann had scored in the 99th percentile, the highest score possible, on her achievement test—produced in black ink. By contrast, the standardized group I.Q. test used to screen candidates for the GT program was printed in purple ink—a problem for someone who suffers from color blindness. A score of at least 120 would have been expected from Beth Ann based on the results of her achievement test. However, because of the ink color, she had trouble completing the test, and scored 89. As a result, she was rejected for the program.

Not satisfied with the ruling of the program coordinator, Gail and I did what just about any parent would have done—we intervened. Based on our own experiences, we knew that an individually administered I.Q. test would be far more reliable than a group administered exam—especially with a student who is sight-impaired. The coordinator resented our refusal to accept the "harsh reality" that our daughter just wasn't as bright as we would like to think; while not quite déjà vu, I wasn't surprised. We pointed out her tremendous performance on the achievement test, and the recommendation by her teacher. The coordinator remained unconvinced. Gail and I stood our ground and insisted on an individually administered test. Knowing we weren't going to take no for an answer, the coordinator relented and gave the test herself. Before commencing with the test, she dismissed our assertion that Beth Ann was sight-impaired and partly color blind—an outrageous position for her to take. Then and there, I realized this person just wasn't very intelligent and resented being challenged.

When the time came for Beth Ann to take the test, Gail and I accompanied her to the testing site and remained nearby throughout the exam. Despite the coordinator's assumption that our daughter would perform poorly, she scored 104. However, this still wasn't high enough to be accepted into the GT program. We didn't believe for a minute that this score was correct, so I requested an appointment to discuss what the final decision would be about Beth Ann's admission to the program.

A few days later, I met with the coordinator one-on-one. I hoped that my own knowledge of the many biases found in standardized tests would help, but unfortunately it did not. The coordinator did finally admit that she had graduated summa cum laude from the master's program at Texas Tech, but had been denied admission into the school's Ph.D. program because of her score on the Graduate Record Exam. She said it was not fair and did not make sense but she still did not understand the analogy and refused to accept Beth Ann into the program.

It was ironic that this woman was so blinded by her own prejudices. That evening, I sat down with Beth Ann and recounted every detail of my visit with the coordinator, who in my opinion was neither gifted nor talented. I assured my daughter that no academic achievement would be off limits to her—including becoming the valedictorian of her high school class. Gail convinced her that remaining in a traditional classroom and taking on extra projects would create an even stronger foundation for her future than participating in a GT program. That fall, Beth Ann was back in the classroom doing what she had always done and always would do—excelling in every subject.

. . .

My focus returned to the bank. The tidal wave I had feared turned out to be very real. Because of oversupply, rig values had plummeted by roughly 80 percent. Rigs that the bank had financed at a cost of $3 million were selling at auction for $600,000. While this was obviously bad for the bank, I did not realize just how bad. Being unfamiliar with the bank's loan portfolio, I would much later learn that the bank had half its assets tied up in loans to purchase drilling rigs. The collateral securing those loans was now woefully inadequate. Unless the bank could raise hundreds of millions of dollars, it would fail.

As far as I knew, the bank's president, chairman of the board, chief operating officer, or board of directors were never even advised of my findings. Even if all these people had known of my concerns at the earliest possible moment, it is unlikely the bank could have been saved. Perhaps the $100 million stock offering recommended by its CFO and me the previous year might have done the trick, but once the rig values began to plummet in early 1982, it was too late. To be sure, the bank's exposure to rig loans was already at a critical level when I joined the bank, but at that time the public-at-large, like me, was unaware of this risk. Consequently, immediate action to raise capital would have been realistic and expected.

On October 14, 1983, the bank became the nation's second largest failure in history, when the Federal Deposit Insurance Corporation (FDIC) declared it insolvent. Its collapse delivered a body blow to the Midland community, and to some degree the entire region. For me and my young family, it portended a major tumult ahead. Even though I had discovered the onrushing tsunami early on, it offered little comfort.

I realized all too well the long-term toll this would exact on Midland. It was abundantly clear that my life would change dramatically—and probably not for the better. The bank's failure could perhaps have been avoided if not for the totalitarian style of its CEO. While I liked him very much and found him always gracious to me, I believe he intimidated the other board members and did not want information from his subordinates that might conflict with his own positions. As far as I could tell, those within his inner circle were afraid to pass along some of our findings and recommendations.

Dumbstruck and filled with grief at the turn of events, I assisted the FDICs bank-closing team in performing the autopsy and securing vital organs. As Gail and I talked about what had happened, I told her that I felt profound regret that the bank failed. However, I also told her that I would do it again in a heartbeat. It had been a wild and wonderful ride.

We knew the Lord still had good things in store for us. Our philosophy remained the same: we would do everything in our power and trust the Lord for the rest. We both realized that I would probably be job hunting before long and doing so against the headwind of a major disability. As always, Gail was my rock.

The acquiring bank, Republic Dallas, said all the right things, but the emotional climate for those of us left behind was still one of postmortem. We all expected to lose our jobs, and each time paychecks were issued, a new list of casualties was announced.

For me, the handwriting was already on the wall. I had been transferred from the marketing department to the credit analysis department six months before the bank failed. My salary was about twice that of the other team members, and I had less credit experience than the rest of the group. My visual impairment rendered me ill-suited for this kind of work. I felt like a low-hanging fruit about to be cut by the staff trimmers.

The layoffs went on through Thanksgiving, Christmas, and into 1984. Toward the end of January, my pastor asked me to address the late service crowd on Brotherhood Sunday, a day that acknowledges the value of laymen in our church. Everyone was keenly aware of the bank's failure and recognized the very real possibility that I might lose my job at any time. In some measure, just about everyone in the community felt a bit less secure about the local economy and the energy industry where their own financial futures were in play. Except for the two percent of Midland County's population involved directly in farming and ranching, everyone who had a job was somehow connected to oil and gas. Teachers, barbers, grocers, and bankers all depended on the energy sector. We were all experiencing a sense of disorder and ambiguity.

My remarks that day described the tremendous sense of disarray and uncertainty in my life, but they also emphasized my conviction that God is a God of incalculable order. I stated my belief that God had a plan for my life, even if I had no idea what that plan might be.

Fortunately, I didn't have to wait long to get an idea about His plan for me—at least His immediate plans for me. The very next day, I was informed that I was no longer an employee of Republic Bank First National Midland—I had been hired by the FDIC. Along with 20 other employees, I was essentially traded to the FDIC. Each of us was given a one-year contract as Local Grade employees (LGs). I was grateful that my salary would actually be slightly higher than my current one.

Gail and I actually laughed at the news because I had just mailed an application for employment to the FDIC the previous Saturday. My hiring occurred before the letter of application had even reached its destination.

I knew this was an act of divine providence—God's provision for us. This appointment would give me time to look for a permanent job. In addition to having a good laugh, Gail and I breathed a sigh of relief.

...

A year passed quickly, and Beth Ann's vision still showed no sign of improving, so we took Dr. Hembree's advice and made an appointment at the Texas Tech Medical School in Lubbock.

Like Dr. Hembree, the neurological ophthalmologist was pleasant, but more importantly, knowledgeable. When I explained that I had always been told that my optic nerve atrophy occurred during my mother's pregnancy and, for that reason, I had no concept of normal vision, he smiled and said the science is very strong now. Those who suffer from this disorder are actually born with normal vision and subsequently experience sight loss in early childhood. This information helped explain why my parents had not detected my sight loss before I entered first grade and why Gail didn't notice Beth Ann's difficulty until she was 5 years old.

The doctor told us of a reliable procedure for determining if someone has optic atrophy. By attaching electrodes to the patient's head and introducing visual stimuli, it is possible to measure the travel time from eye to brain. We consented to the procedure, even though we knew it would be grueling. Beth Ann began to cry when the electrodes were attached to her head; the apparatus was about as comfortable as a crown of thorns. When the procedure was complete, the verdict was clear. The travel time from her eyes to her brain was three times the normal span. Moreover, he assessed her visual acuity as ranging from 20/60 to 20/80, or one-third to one-fourth of normal. My heart sank. Mercifully, this physician didn't offer the pronouncement that I had heard those many years ago while a junior high student—that there is no hope that your vision will ever improve. Although I was close enough to my child's face to see her expression, there was no way of knowing if the tears and red face reflected only the discomfort of the procedure or if she realized at that moment the long-term implications of the doctor's remarks. The only good news was that her impairment was only about one-tenth as severe as mine, and the damage to her vision was almost surely over.

He asked to also examine Becky. We were surprised by his request, given that we really didn't feel it was necessary—but we agreed. The outcome for Becky was the same as for Beth Ann—except her sight loss was not as pronounced. Her visual acuity was measured at 20/40. The distinction between the two levels of visual acuity was significant. As long as Becky sat in the front half of the classroom, she would be able to see the chalkboard. By contrast, unless the teacher was writing directly in front of her, in bold characters and using highly contrasting colors, Beth Ann would not be able to see the chalkboard—even if she was sitting in the front row. Becky would have no trouble passing the visual exam for a driver's license—her sister would have great difficulty. Both girls had to do their schoolwork, such as reading and writing, from a closer proximity and with more effort than others. Not surprisingly, neither of them has ever read just for pleasure.

Even though Becky's optic atrophy was present when she was tested at age 5, the damage had run its course by that time, and she experienced no further sight loss. For Beth Ann, it was devastating news, but at last we finally knew what we were dealing with. Decades of pronouncements by countless eye care professionals assuring me that my disorder was not hereditary had been flat-out wrong. Now that her impairment was documented, the public school system would be notified so they could accommodate any special needs she might have. Even so, not many things changed. When Beth Ann entered fourth grade in 1985, the extent of her accommodation was getting dark-printed copies of handouts and tests. Her schoolwork continued to be excellent, and she drew little attention from her teachers or school administrators. We decided that is how it should be.

The whole episode with both our daughters' diminished vision, especially for Beth Ann, whose life would be significantly impacted, caused many emotions in me and in Gail. For one thing, I had assured Gail before we married that there were no risks of any of our children inheriting my disease, and I felt badly about that. Also, I resented the uniformly incorrect information I had been given by professionals I trusted. I hated the realization that Beth Ann, in particular, would have to suffer many of the hardships against which I had struggled, presumably for the rest of her life. She and Becky would now be confronted with the specter of possibly passing along the genetic poison.

Gail, who had been a stay-at-home mother while the girls were small, returned to work as a second grade teacher in the fall of 1985. Given my tenuous job situation, we both felt it was the prudent thing to do—plus, Gail was ready. Even though we didn't know it at the time, her reputation would grow over time, producing honors none of us were expecting. At that time, she was simply doing what she had always done and always has done—everything in her power to help our family. Her help meant so very much—she minimized the considerable stress caused by the frustrations I was experiencing while trying to fit in at the FDIC.

CHAPTER 16

GOOD FORTUNE

As I began to think about my new position, I wondered if my disability would prevent me from fitting in and performing well. I wasn't even sure the FDIC knew about my disability at the time they included me in the draft. Certainly, there was no reason to suspect I was selected because of my disability. In 1984, we were still a half-dozen years away from the Americans with Disabilities Act (ADA).

The idea of starting a new job not knowing a single FDIC employee was unsettling. While I knew the 19 bank employees who had also transitioned over, we were quickly scattered among the various departments that had been set up to liquidate more than $900 million of assets from the failed bank.

As I always had, I dealt with this uncertainty with confidence. This was my own psychological adaptation of the "get thee behind me Satan" principle, and explains why my favorite line from *The Sound of Music* is, "I have confidence in confidence alone."

I settled in and began working on a portfolio of loans acquired by the FDIC. Frankly, a lot of what I was doing was clerical, and seemed a waste of my skills, especially given my salary. I learned that the FDIC had looked at the salary being paid to each of us by Republic Bank, and moved each one to the next higher pay grade. While my view was that a significant portion of our work could have been done by very competent secretaries, I was grateful that I had a job at the salary I was receiving, even if it was not especially intellectually motivating.

The inability to scan quickly had always been one of my biggest limitations when using a viewer. To understand this limitation, consider the way normally sighted people glance all over the left and right sides of an open newspaper to search for topics of interest to them. Now imagine trying to do that using a handheld magnifying glass. If, on the other hand, someone handed me a newspaper with a finger placed at the beginning of an article of interest to me, I could read every word, no matter how small the print. The problem was that I was expected to scan materials all day, every day.

I hated being at such a competitive disadvantage. My father had instilled in me a sense of urgency and a need to work not only hard, but fast. It seemed as if the major ingredient in my lifelong strategy to compete in a world of people with normal sight was my ability to adapt and exceed expectations. As the turtle in a race of hares, I had always found ways of making up lost time. Through the years, nothing had made me feel more insecure than being slow at something—at anything. Figuring out how to make myself valuable in this environment was going to be a huge challenge, and there was no obvious opportunity for me to grab onto.

The physical office environment didn't do much to motivate me—it was drab and dreary; nothing like the bank. By now, it was apparent that I was visually impaired but the FDIC failed to acknowledge my special needs and address them. Each of us was handed a stack of legal-length folders filled with hundreds of pages of bank documents and left to our own devices. Seven small metal desks had been crammed into an area originally intended as a hall: four along one wall and three along the other. There were not enough outlets for phones and electrical devices for all the desks, let alone a place to set up my viewer. To function properly, I needed an L-shaped desk or one with a credenza beside or behind it, but no such provision was made, even after explaining my challenges. Remember, these were the days before the ADA—organizations weren't obligated to make accommodations.

The entire environment reeked of mindlessness—no one seemed to want to take advantage of my experience and skills. I spoke candidly with the Lord about this, explaining that I trusted that He still had a plan for my life but assured Him that I didn't have a clue how the pieces could add up to anything.

I decided I would just have to find ways of adapting to the circumstances as they existed, and began by requesting work that was complicated and involved a lot of money. I successfully argued that this would allow the FDIC to take advantage of my intellectual skills and experience.

Before long, I had an opportunity to offer a suggestion which, if implemented, could be applied anywhere in the country where the FDIC was engaged in salvaging money from failed banks—not just in the Midland office. The head of the Midland office, known as the Liquidator in Charge (LIC), called a meeting so he could solicit recommendations for improving the office's operations. I wanted to get noticed and use this as an opportunity to stand out, so I spoke up first. My idea was to use experienced secretaries as paraprofessionals. The LIC described my idea as "stupid," publicly humiliating me. I remember thinking there is something stupid here, but it wasn't my suggestion. I was dumbstruck by his obvious lack of leadership. Even more alarming to me was his response to an idea offered in good faith—it displayed a lack of basic human decency. After my suggestion was lambasted, no one else raised a hand, and the meeting ended.

Coincidentally, just a few months later, the division implemented the use of "super secretaries" who could function as paraprofessionals. I never received any recognition.

The brutal response to my suggestion was an omen. I soon realized that it wasn't just this one manager—I quickly noticed a pattern. Senior-level managers were all longtime FDIC employees, which meant virtually all of them had been bank examiners—thus, accountants. In practical terms, this meant they had no real experience in liquidation. They were great at sifting through oceans of paperwork and finding nuggets of accounting insights useful in assessing a bank's financial strength. With few exceptions, they had spent their careers working alone in small, out-of-the-way rooms in the banks they were evaluating. They spent their careers figuring out what needed to be fixed—and instructing others to fix it. Now they were being asked to oversee a completely different type of operation, and it took a while for most of them to retool their mind-sets. Consequently, they were looking for people who were whizzes at scanning through large volumes of paper to understand the value of what it was the FDIC now owned and needed to salvage. In this environment, I did not consider my future very bright. This was at least the sixth time I had undertaken a challenge when those in charge had very low expectations of me. Each time, I had gotten off to a rocky start, yet each time I accomplished my goals by a wide margin. Because the pathway for repeating this pattern was totally hidden from me during my early months at the FDIC, I decided that my goal was to make it through 12 months. At the end of one year, I would be evaluated and renewed or terminated—the latter was not a great option, so I needed to change perceptions about me quickly.

Because bank failures were relatively rare at that time, the FDIC was experiencing growing pains. All of a sudden, highly skilled technicians accustomed to working independently were thrust into the limelight. As evidenced by my own experience making a suggestion, most had no leadership experience, and struggled as a result.

We would all have to adapt. I ended up putting both my MBA training and credit analysis experience to good use. All of us seemed to have one thing in common—trying to figure out what our jobs were. Once again, my confidence helped me adapt.

After a few months, my manager resigned, and I applied for his position. Another candidate, with far fewer qualifications than I had, got the job, and I was not the least surprised. I had been passed over twice at city hall, where I believed the mayor's wishes took precedence over those of the city manager. Whether my disability figured in his excluding me I never knew. It was more likely the result of old-fashioned politics. At the bank, I was also passed over. Once again, there was no way of being sure to what extent my disability may have played a role, as the candidate selected was certainly well-qualified. At church, the prejudice was easier to see. When the long-range planning committee was established, someone with no planning credentials was asked to be its chairman. When two leaders were needed to head the young adult department, I was relegated to the number two position. For years I was passed over as a candidate for deacon, a circumstance that was not remedied until my ascension to a more prestigious position at the bank helped folks see me in a different light. Many people have a great deal of difficulty envisioning a person with a disability as someone who can be in charge. Ironically, the magnitude of this kind of bias became especially clear when I began to serve on the boards of various organizations for the disabled.

I began receiving invitations to serve as chairman or president from a variety of organizations. About this time, my level of involvement in civic and church activities reached an all-time high of 13. I was either president or committee chairman for every group that represented, or supported, disabled persons. Interestingly, Gail noticed that when an organization was not focused on the disabled, I was never seriously considered for either of these positions—even though I was clearly the unofficial leader of several of those groups. I was sought after as the person with the greatest technical expertise and as someone capable of generating an endless stream of ideas—but never officially sanctioned.

It had always been enough to know I was making a contribution to a worthwhile enterprise. However, that didn't mean that the discrimination against me didn't hurt—I was thoroughly frustrated by it. I never once voiced a protest because I was afraid others would see me as arrogant or bitter. Prejudice is the ultimate blind spot. It is itself a disability. Martin Luther King Jr. dreamed of a day when "a person shall be judged not by the color of his skin but by the content of his character." I began to dream of a day when a person's fitness to contribute and lead would be measured not by his proximity to the norm but by his capacity to exceed the norm.

Sometimes, as in my case, pushing back against the perceived potential for prejudice can impact your personality in ways that reduce your appeal to others. There is an intensity about me that attracts most people, but puts off others. Through aging and lots of dedicated coaching by Gail, I am getting better at my goal of always being gentle. So, I am not only dreaming of the day when prejudice toward disabled persons is a thing of the past, but one in which disabled persons no longer hurt their own causes by responding inappropriately.

No matter how vivid my dream of such a day, I had to deal with the present reality. I decided to focus on what I could control. If I couldn't be a commander, I would become the best soldier I could. Fortunately, the front line of attack in my division could be fought with a pen, so I was well armed for battle.

Almost all decisions made by the Division of Liquidation required a written case be approved by a designated person or committee. A case was essentially a report outlining your recommendations and the reasons for those recommendations. The most difficult case to get approved was one seeking authority to settle for less than full payment. The larger the debt forgiveness requested, the more difficult the struggle to get approval.

Despite the slow pace at which I was able to work, I managed to negotiate a huge compromise. This case became the Midland office's first compromise case to be approved at the Washington Committee level—a very big deal. One reason it was such a big deal was that it argued for the FDIC to release a debtor on a $6 million loan for a one-time payment of roughly 12 percent of that figure. There was a heavy burden of proof on my shoulders to establish that the offer on the table was the best deal that could be struck. Having prepared the case, which won praise at both the Dallas and Washington offices, established me as the premier case-writer in the Midland office.

I went on to receive an extraordinarily high set of marks during my first annual performance review. Shortly thereafter, I got a letter from our office's director of personnel congratulating me on having been selected to receive a three-year appointment. While this was certainly a relief since I had not been successful in finding other work, it still wasn't the position I wanted and I was still a contract employee, meaning I received no retirement benefits. With Gail's help, I continued to look for another position outside of the FDIC.

Looking for a job is an arduous process for anyone; for someone with a disability, it can be exacerbated many times. From the very beginning, I wondered if I should disclose my disability and address it in a positive way as an illustration of my strengths. Or would that disqualify me before I even had an interview? If I were completely upfront, I knew I would receive fewer responses, but the ones I did get would be serious ones. I chose to disclose.

I know now that I made the wrong decision in revealing my disability. I never once received a reply, not even an acknowledgment. Although I have no proof, I believe that many of the persons who received my applications thought it safer to ignore them than to even acknowledge receipt. Even pre-ADA, organizations were concerned they would face litigation if they interviewed someone with a disability, and decided not to hire them. Simply pretending they never received the application was how they dealt with the issue. It was clear to me fear of litigation for perceived violations of laws and/ or the failure to meet quotas prevented me from getting interviews. In fact, the director of personnel at the Midland office advised me not to disclose my disability when submitting job applications.

The most shocking aspect of my hypothesis is that if I were them, I would probably have done the very same thing. Quotas have proven to be a double-edged sword. In some ways, they have benefited victims of prejudice; in other ways they have hurt them. I am not a fan of quotas; to me, they have the potential to keep the most qualified person from being hired, but I have to admit that they have been a powerful tool in combating something worse than quotas—discrimination. When efforts to liberate one group from discrimination result in introducing discrimination in another group or class, something isn't working right.

In the end, after all the buzzwords and catchy phrases of politicians have been pronounced and the lofty assertions of academicians have been articulated, quotas are about who will be granted economic opportunity and who will not—it is that simple. I know from my own experience. Physical attributes should never trump qualifications. I consider it immoral to consider anything other than a job applicant's relevant qualifications.

The way I felt about this period of applying but never receiving an acknowledgment reflected what I believed. I still felt that God was involved in all that was going on, or not going on. I decided to evaluate my experience and skills to see if I might catch a glimpse of the Lord's plan for me. In an epiphany, it came to me: I had the perfect background to be a church planner. Having served for several years on my own church's long-range planning committee, I had gotten a good look at what was needed. A strong background in city and regional planning and a strong background in banking and debt planning was what was needed, along with strong communication skills.

No one I'd ever known in the field of planning had been so perfectly groomed to conduct church planning. I believed this was no accident, but part of the Lord's plan for me. Through much prayer and creative energy, a plan of action soon emerged. Jim Sellers, a friend and fellow deacon in my church who had just lost his job, could bring creditability to my efforts—and as an engineer, analytical skills. More important, he was a person of great conviction about the Lord's work, and was also looking for direction.

In the summer of 1985, we decided to coauthor a workbook that focused on church planning. By early October of that year we completed the sample chapters, and approached a publisher. While we waited for their response, we had the opportunity to serve as consultants to the First Baptist Church of Grapevine, Texas. Our goal was to produce a Cadillac-quality master plan that we could use as a promotional tool. Over the next several months, Jim and I devoted roughly 1,000 hours to the development and refinement of the Grapevine plan. Even though we realized very little for our efforts, our primary goal was to have a plan we could show to other churches.

During the time we developed the plan, I received a promotion and pay raise at the FDIC. While I appreciated the recognition and the money, I still felt my position there was on a road leading nowhere. I had no expectation of being at the FDIC long-term so I was anxious to develop another career path. After the plan was finished, we tried marketing our services to other churches but had no budget for advertising. Having to rely on letter writing and a few in-person visits, we were unable to generate any business. Although we did some city planning and zoning work, along with real estate consulting for individuals and firms, the venture wasn't sustainable. The partnership ended on good terms. The techniques we developed and the information we gained allowed me to help other churches later on. After having invested roughly 13,000 hours of spare time in writing and preparing four workbooks on church planning, along with actual church planning, I ended my dream of being a church planner. Wasting hundreds of hours trying to help a church whose pastor believed that God speaks only to the senior pastor by implanting some type of ephemeral impression was the last straw.

By that time, I had been selected to assist the other 87 account officers in writing effective cases, an assignment that lasted for another eight months. I was then sent back to my department and, once again, given a portfolio. During the first year of managing this portfolio, I collected enough money to pay the salaries and benefits of every account officer in the Midland office.

Once again, I decided to pursue entry-level management positions within the FDIC. Once again, I was frustrated. After six months and a multitude of rejections, I was convinced that I was traveling down a dead-end street. Finally, in May of 1987, I became exasperated and wrote a note to myself about the hopelessness I felt on my copy of one of the applications I had completed. I wondered if I would ever get ahead while at the FDIC, or continue to get rejected. This hit home especially hard because the available position was one vacated by the sudden death of my immediate supervisor and section chief. I felt strongly that I was the most qualified candidate, but still got passed over.

The Lord obviously had other plans for me. Shortly after this latest disappointment, I got a phone call from the number two official in the Midland office. He instructed me to come to his office for a meeting with him and the head of the commercial loans department. I had been summoned to discuss my interest in accepting a management position in the commercial real estate area. I was told I had not been selected for the previous position I applied for because I was needed in real estate.

The section I would be responsible for contained the worst credits in the building. They were old credits secured by badly depreciated real estate. Moreover, the section had been failing under the manager I was to replace.

I couldn't believe my good fortune; I accepted the position and dove in headfirst. Almost immediately, the performance of the section accelerated dramatically and measurably. Just about when I was ready to prepare a memo to my boss and his boss pointing out the 60 percent increase in average monthly case production and corresponding increase in collections, my boss' boss resigned. This left me feeling vulnerable because the person who handpicked me for the position was now gone. There was no one I could trust to backstop my immediate boss, whose competency and scruples I had long questioned.

Before long a new division head arrived to replace the one who had resigned. A couple of months later, the year ended, and my boss was asked by his new supervisor to explain why collections for the year were down in my section, as compared to the previous year. I asked whether he had mentioned the fact that average monthly collections for the last seven months of the year—the months since my appointment—surpassed those for the first five months by 55 percent. I asked if he explained that we had begun the year in question with one-third fewer loans to work. Although he lacked the guts to admit it, he had completely dropped the ball, and lacked the courage to set the record straight. Realizing this, I informed him of my plans to explain these facts myself. He ordered me not to discuss the matter with his boss. Instead, he allowed his boss to go on thinking that my performance had been substandard. What followed was a barrage of attacks on my capability, all launched by the division head but instigated by my boss.

It reached the point that my boss was deliberately undercutting my authority with my team by calling in one of my subordinates for consultation and assigning him responsibilities that should have been mine. The untenable nature of this situation ate at me day and night. Finally, after a couple of sleepless nights, I developed a plan, formulated out of fear, because I knew I could be terminated at the drop of a hat or my contract simply not renewed. The threat was even greater for me as a disabled person because finding another job would have been much more difficult and time-consuming. Clearly, I was being bullied and knew it. A number of people saw what was taking place and resented it. In fact, a couple of my attorney friends who worked with the FDIC urged me to sue and expressed an eagerness to take some of the action. They had seen enough firsthand to believe it would be a rout, with me emerging as the victor. Convinced that I was being bullied because I was disabled, I was sure I could win a discrimination suit and emerge with more money than my family would ever need. The drawer full of rejected requests for advancement where less qualified individuals had been selected over me would speak for itself. Moreover, it would be easy to document that I was being tormented into resigning my position. My attorney friends joked about how much they would enjoy getting me on the witness stand and exposing my brilliance and work ethic, and the discrimination I had suffered. However, I would do so only if terminated or if I continued to be harassed. I offered a peaceful solution. I would forfeit my management position and return to my old department as an account officer.

After presenting my plan, I was offered a compromise. I would stay in the commercial department but under the supervision of someone I considered the ablest and most respectable section chief I knew, Doug Woodward.

Under Doug's direction, I immediately began to challenge the most productive case writers in the department. Later that year, the top two management spots at the Midland office were vacated and then filled. The two new managers, Bob Longworth and Don Allen, were wonderful. Bob, in particular, was good about dropping in on the account officers in their offices just to show an interest in the work that we were doing. He quickly took a special interest in my techniques and results.

Soon, Bob asked me if I would establish a program to teach new account officers and do it on a full-time basis. I responded enthusiastically but asked to keep my portfolio, arguing that I could do both. Bob and Don agreed. Working passionately, I designed a curriculum and composed a full-length training manual. Although it had taken five years, once again I had turned a rocky start into a wonderful situation. Gone were the senior managers who completely overlooked my skills because of their preconceived notions about the limitations of my sight impairment. My supervisor was perhaps the most brilliant person I had encountered at any level at the FDIC. He was well-qualified, but more importantly, he recognized my gifts and was not threatened by them. Like any good manager, he strove to empower me to do my best. Although I had taken pride in and mostly enjoyed my work since the end of my first year, things were now at a whole new level. Just maybe, I thought, there is actually a permanent home for me at the FDIC.

CHAPTER 17

SENSE OF DESTINY

Up to and including my first six years at the FDIC, we did our best to just live a normal life. Gail had been back in the classroom for five years when the new George H.W. Bush Elementary School opened in Midland. As was the custom when a new school opened, one outstanding teacher was named from each of the existing schools to staff the new one. Gail was chosen by her principal for the honor.

Becky moved seamlessly from preschool to fifth grade, despite coping with less than perfect eyesight and what would later be diagnosed as Attention Deficit Disorder (ADD). While she could take one or two pieces of information and make lightning-fast deductions from it, her teachers noticed a disconnect when she needed to apply a large number of facts to gain an overview. Eventually, a psychologist diagnosed the disorder and prescribed a medication that proved very helpful. We would discover years later that her mental makeup was better suited for a college student than a public school pupil because of the need for significant breaks during the day.

During junior high, Beth Ann started working with the district's new low vision coordinator. This woman was generally helpful, but she made one wrong assumption. She demanded that Gail and I stop pushing Beth Ann to earn all As. She didn't bother to ask if we were pushing. Instead, she misinterpreted our conviction that expectations should not be lowered for Beth Ann because she had trouble seeing. As parents, we wanted her to understand that she could achieve whatever she wanted to achieve. Beth Ann had no intention of downsizing her aspirations to fit some preconceived notion, and we wanted to make it clear to this woman that our family would not expect less of someone because they had a disability. We let her know that Beth Ann was the one doing the pushing; that she had no intention of accepting anything below an A and knew she could do it. Gail took issue with the coordinator's inference that falling a little short of excellence would somehow prepare Beth Ann for disappointing results in the future. For us as parents, and for me as someone who had overcome incredible obstacles, the idea that having to overcome hardships builds character was no justification for lowering the bar now. Our child had been overcoming hardships since age 5, and we wanted to be sure she grew up with the confidence to deal with any obstacles she may face in life.

Gail and I wanted to help Beth Ann avoid the pitfalls I had encountered when forced to take algebra for the first time in college: the extreme frustration and humiliation I suffered trying to learn the material without the benefit of seeing either the chalkboard or the textbook. Beth Ann could read a normal print book, and see the chalkboard if she were close enough. We wanted to be sure she would not feel intimidated in the future, especially when it came to math. Gail spoke to the coordinator for mathematics at Midland ISD, who suggested we find a gifted teacher to serve as her tutor. The tutor we hired told us: "I don't know why you hired me. Beth Ann is consistently doing A+ work for me." By the middle of ninth grade, Beth Ann had firmly established herself as one of the top students in her math class. This would continue to occur repeatedly throughout high school. Her success in algebra, the one subject that had given me such grief, reflected the main differences in our educational experiences: Though well below normal, her eyesight was roughly 10 times as good as mine. She began the study of algebra in the ninth grade rather than as a college student who was presumed to have had a foundation in the subject during high school. Gail and I had always advocated for both of our children. Beth Ann knew we thought she was extremely intelligent and could learn anything. My parents were just glad I found a way to make it from one year to the next. There was never any doubt in our minds that Beth Ann was an exceptionally bright person, so we treated as complete rubbish the bogus I.Q. scores that had apparently led her low vision teacher to think we were asking too much of her academically.

During this time, I was nominated to receive the 1989 Presidential Award for Most Outstanding Federal Employee with Disabilities, an extraordinary honor. In the history of the FDIC, no employee had received this honor. Ultimately, the nomination went to another well-deserving person, a woman with cystic fibrosis who then went on to be chosen for a Presidential Award. I was happy for her, and thrilled that my work had been recognized in such a way.

The next year I was nominated again by the Midland office. This time I was selected to represent the FDIC in the competition with all other federal civilian and military agencies. I was selected to receive a Presidential Award, and could scarcely believe it. I might as well have won an Oscar!

As soon as I heard the news, I phoned Gail to tell her the good news. She told me how proud she was for me. I had to choke back the tears, as I remembered the same comment she had made a year earlier, when I was nominated for the award.

I considered the award my gift to Gail for believing in me. In December of 1990, the entire family traveled to Washington, D.C., where we were treated like royalty for five of the most glorious days of our lives.

When Marilyn Quayle, wife of then Vice President Dan Quayle, learned that our daughter Beth Ann became ill during the night and was unable to attend the awards ceremony, she wrote her a sweet note inside a program. What I especially recall was Mrs. Quayle's empathy. Perhaps she had a life-changing experience like the one I had with my own sister, Janie.

After being honored by Mrs. Quayle and the other dignitaries, Gail, Becky, and I accompanied all those in attendance to a luncheon given in our honor, where I was presented an American flag that had been flown over the nation's capital in my honor on November 14, 1990.

That day, during an interview, I was asked to describe what receiving the Presidential Award meant to me. I said that it meant many things but these were the three most important: I was thankful for the opportunity to provide that moment and honor to my wife, who had believed in me when things looked a lot different—at that point, the reporter conducting the interview actually began to cry. I said that my wish was that a disabled youngster would look at me and say that he or she would like to be like me. Finally, I said that I hoped my receiving a Presidential Award would help my girls, Beth Ann and Becky, embrace for themselves a sense of the possible—*a sense of destiny.*

CHAPTER 18

WILL AND WAY

We returned from Washington, D.C., to a hero's welcome in Midland that was both unexpected and touching. The local television station featured the event on the news the evening we returned, and a party was held in my honor when I returned to the office the next day.

As 1990 drew to a close, my family and I felt a very keen sense of God's providence and His blessings in leading me to the FDIC. At that time, and for years to come, the organization grew rapidly—not only in numbers of employees, but in terms of the organization's understanding of the human spirit. In the immediate aftermath of the award, it seemed as though the shackles of negative stereotyping had fallen away from me and my career at the FDIC. In its place, there seemed to exist a corporate-wide recognition of my skills and dedication to the organization. Virtually every FDIC employee in the country knew my name and viewed me with respect. All indications were that a 180-degree turn had occurred in my career prospects at the FDIC. So long as I remained in the Midland office, my expectations were validated.

As our nation continued to make progress in its response to persons with disabilities, the federal government led the way. In fact, the very person who signed my Presidential Award was the same person who had, earlier that year, signed into law the ADA to prevent discrimination against individuals with disabilities in the areas of employment, transportation, public accommodations, and telecommunications—President George H.W. Bush. The FDIC moved to the forefront in this area, especially with the administration of Chairman William Seidman. This maturation process certainly benefited me, at least in the short term, and I would like to think I contributed in some small way to the FDIC's awakening to the potential contributions of individuals with disabilities. What I did not anticipate was the ability of one person to undermine the firm's new, more enlightened intentions. For the time being, things could not have been better.

In early 1991, the manual I had written was officially inducted into the FDIC's resource library in Washington, D.C. I was invited to audit the teaching of my manual for a week in the New Brunswick, New Jersey, office that March. While in New Jersey, I called Beth Downs, the English teacher who had meant so much to me during high school. Every year, I made it a point of wishing her a happy birthday. As I explained the reason for my trip to the New Jersey office, she began to laugh. For the first time in many such phone visits, she revealed that she had been warned about me at the outset: "Every time I need a good laugh, I just recall having been told that you were a stupid kid." This revelation was shocking to me, but Mrs. Downs steadfastly refused to name the school official who had so missed the mark in judging me. I was stunned that any teacher who possessed the slightest understanding of the obstacles that confronted me could have considered me stupid. Oddly enough, instead of feeling anger or vindictiveness, I began to speculate about what could have led to such a perception. If such a judgment could be made about the learning potential of someone who would later be found to possess a genius I.Q., what about children who didn't necessarily have that level of intelligence? Would they be forgotten and simply tossed aside? Physical disabilities have no bearing on intelligence. The I.Q. scores of 100 sight-impaired individuals are likely to mirror that of any 100 non-sight-impaired persons in the general population. However, such parity only becomes clear when extra care is taken to remove biases from the I.Q. tests administered to visually impaired individuals.

I had long thought of my public school persona as the "Camouflage Kid." My gifts had been so obscured against the backdrop of my classroom ineptness as to be visible only by the very few, like Mrs. Downs. I wondered how many of my teachers had misjudged me or any other disabled student because we were different. What, if anything, could be done to preempt the development and spread of such contaminated judgments? I wondered if I might be able to do something to break this cycle of disaster.

When I returned to Texas, I learned that the Midland office was going to be closed. The FDIC executive sent to Midland asked for my help in evaluating the closing. My familiarity with public officials at the local level was well-known, so my help was sought in identifying and inviting key officials to meet with. Intended or not, I actively assumed the role of advocate for retaining the office and encouraged community leaders to discuss the impact that closing the office would have on the community. Unfortunately, our efforts failed.

I was invited to relocate to San Antonio to be the training administrator. Although the training position and working for Bob Longworth again both appealed to me, I passed on the offer because that office was likely to close in a few years. Gail and I did not want to force the girls to pull up stakes twice during their school years. By contrast, the Dallas regional office offered a much greater sense of permanence. In July of 1991, I caught an early flight from Midland to Dallas to check out my new digs. Five weeks later, Gail and the girls joined me.

Moving from Midland was very difficult for us. Gail was raised there, the girls had never lived anywhere else, and I had invested 20 years directly and indirectly trying to improve the city's future. Leaving Midland meant moving away from Gail's mother and most of our friends. It also meant that, for the first time since she graduated from college, Gail had to actively look for a job. In the past, because of her experience and reputation as the Coordinator of Early Childhood in Midland, all she had to do was let someone know she was available. Gail also had to give up the home we had built, cared for, and loved. Finally, it meant giving up Crestview Baptist Church, including the couples Sunday school class we had taught for nine years.

Even though we were leaving so much behind, we had a great sense of optimism about what God had planned for us in the Metroplex, the area in north Texas that is made up of roughly 100 towns and cities including Dallas, Fort Worth, Arlington, Carrollton, Plano, and McKinney. Generally speaking, it's difficult to know when you leave one city and enter another because they have grown together. The Trinity River snakes its way through much of this four-county area, and lakes, streams, and ponds abound, as does the variety of trees and topographic features. Midland, like much of west Texas, is flat and dry, and its natural vegetation is sparse and uninspiring—the opposite of our new home.

Very quickly, exciting things took place. Gail was hired by the most prestigious school district in the Metroplex, and the girls adjusted well to their new schools. We even managed to build a nicer home than the one we left behind.

When I was interviewed about receiving the Presidential Award, I told the interviewer, "It is important for people to understand that a person with a sensory impairment can experience a life of joy and fulfillment." At that moment, my life was indeed full of joy and fulfillment. I liked who I was and what I was doing. I adored my wife, and could not imagine two more wonderful daughters than Beth Ann and Becky. These women were, and still are, among the great constants in my life. Then, as now, much of my time is spent enjoying and enhancing these relationships.

My work at the FDIC, combined with other creative outlets, challenged me as God's plans for me unfolded. From a long-term perspective, I planned to continue writing journal articles and possibly other books as well. I thought about establishing a department for urban and church studies at a major church-sponsored university. I felt I had reached a mile-marker in my career, mile-marker 45. I had turned 45 that year, but I also felt that this was a logical time for reflecting and looking ahead. The time was right for me to look back down the road behind me and see the evidence of God's participation in my life. It was a time for reaping the fruits of much labor and many struggles. As always, it was a time for dreaming and making plans.

Little did I know there was a struggle ahead of me throughout the balance of my career at the FDIC. The struggle ahead would be against a foe that I presumed had been conquered before I arrived in Dallas. Unfortunately, there are people out there who are intent on resurrecting barriers that others have tried to tear down. The deputy regional director effectively reconstructed the glass ceiling that bedeviled me early in my career. As one of his direct reports put it in a book he wrote after leaving the FDIC, this person had "caused many a subordinate to reevaluate their career options."

The deputy director of the regional office did not share the director's admiration for me or even a sense of respect. In fact, he seemed to take pleasure in making sure I did not think more of myself than he thought I should. Since college, he had done nothing but work for the FDIC, primarily as a bank examiner. There can be no question that this individual had paid his dues at the FDIC, including countless days and nights away from his family, often staying in cheap hotels in obscure locations. I couldn't help but think that he resented those of us who had not made the same sacrifices he had. Whether his measures to block my advancement grew out of a prejudice against disabled persons is hard to say. To be sure, he was anything but a people person.

At this time, there was an emphasis on promoting women. The effort to promote women was done in a mindless way—instead of hiring/promoting them based on their qualifications, it was obvious they were being hired to fulfill a quota. The Dallas office was singled out as having a low proportion of female executives compared to males. In my experience, when you focus on providing preferential treatment to one group, another group is placed at a disadvantage. My view on quotas is simple: factors such as race, gender, religious beliefs, disability, and sexual orientation should never be allowed to trump qualifications—if they do, we invite institutional discrimination. On more than one occasion, the position of regional training administrator became available; each time I was overlooked. The last time I expressed my interest in the position, I barely got out my first sentence when the deputy director began telling me how extraordinarily capable another hire was. He made sure she stayed in the position of acting regional training administrator for a year so she would meet the minimum qualifications to apply for the job. At this, the personnel director became outraged and confronted the deputy director, and immediately resigned in protest. The personnel director told me the Dallas office had been criticized for having too few female executives. He admitted to me that decisions to hire and particularly to promote less-qualified candidates had been made in order to placate those in Washington. Before long, a pattern of promoting less qualified candidates in order to fill a quota became clear. Only after I had been passed over for the one position that I felt uniquely qualified to hold did I realize that hiring managers were being encouraged to discriminate in the form of filling a quota—in this case, ironically, against males. As the father of two very capable girls, I never wanted either of them discriminated against or given an opportunity simply because of their sex—it makes no sense.

At that point, I surrendered all hope for advancement at the FDIC.

Despite the atmosphere, my work continued to be fulfilling, and I continued to receive outstanding annual performance evaluations and decent raises. Thankfully, my performance evaluations were done by supervisors who actually observed my day-to-day work.

In January of 1995, after about three and a half years at the Dallas office, I shared an assignment with Susan Kilgore, an exceptionally capable real estate attorney. We met via a conference call with a very frustrated debtor who was in desperate straits. Together we quickly cleaned up a mess created by a higher-ranking official. Our actions allowed this dying man to put his financial affairs in order within the very short time he had left to live. Before the call ended, I had proposed a series of initiatives that could resolve his obligations to the FDIC, including a legal component which Susan quickly embraced. Despite the jokes about working for the FDIC centering on foreclosing on widows and orphans, I rejoiced at opportunities to help another human being and his family. I also felt satisfaction at achieving the best outcome for the FDIC—it truly was a "win-win."

Immediately after we ended our conference call, Susan called me to express her appreciation for the skill I had used and said she would like to invite me to the next meeting of a Toastmasters Club. She dropped by my office and escorted me to the meeting room and introduced me to the club members, who, I would soon learn, were in the process of securing a charter for their club. At that very first meeting, I was called upon to participate as a contestant in an activity called table topics. The rules seemed straightforward enough: Each participant is asked to discuss a topic for not less than one minute and no longer than two. There would be zero time between when the topic would be announced and when I was supposed to stand and begin speaking. Right away, I liked this new game. In fact, I became the club's first president, and eventually earned the right to represent the club in table topics competitions held at bigger venues.

Toastmasters was more than an interesting pastime and an outlet for advancement not available to me at the FDIC. It addressed the goal I had had since high school: "To become a sculptor of elegant thoughts both as a writer and speaker." Even more important, honing my public speaking skills could lead to a career as a motivational speaker once my career at the FDIC was over. Public speaking had been an important part of my career activities since my earliest days at the regional planning commission. However, Toastmasters allowed me to compete against other speakers and learn from them. Preparing myself for any opportunity to write or speak to general audiences had never stopped being important to me.

...

In January 1999, Daddy was diagnosed with lung cancer and given six months to live. For 41 of the next 42 weekends, I would travel to Mineral Wells. Every Friday, I would carry a suitcase to work on the 6:30 a.m. express to downtown and take the bus to Mineral Wells after lunch. On Sunday mornings, I would return home to Carrollton. Often, Gail would come to get me—sometimes meeting me in Weatherford or Fort Worth and having lunch with whatever family members had driven me that far.

During that 10-month period, I helped my father put his affairs in order. I restored and painted an old duplex my parents had rented out for 40 years. My father wanted to sell it so my mother would have the cash instead of the headaches of being a landlord. Several of my old Tarleton buddies came up to help. I will always be thankful for the time I had to say goodbye. Mercifully, Daddy's mind remained sharp until three days before he passed, when the lack of oxygen to his brain began to manifest itself. Although he outlived the forecast by four months, once he began to decline, the end came sooner than I had expected. On Friday, November 19, 1999, it became necessary to transport him to the hospital, so I returned home Sunday afternoon. I wanted to go into the office Monday morning to put matters in order, so I could be gone the next week.

My brother had been at the hospital about 10 p.m. to honor our father's request for a shave. Shortly after returning home, he got the call. One of the greatest intellects and most compassionate individuals I had ever known was gone. I was comforted by those family and friends who were able to attend the service, including several of my old Tarleton friends. After the funeral, Mama headed straight for her piano and began playing familiar hymns. For the 50 years beginning with Janie's illness right through Daddy's declining months that piano had been her constant friend, distraction, and comfort. Somehow, I knew she would be okay.

...

I returned to Carrollton. For the next four or five years, the Ashby clan continued to work hard and reach new milestones. Becky was thriving at a community college, far more than she had in high school. Limiting her class hours to an hour or two a day left her with large gaps in her day and worked much better with her ADD. She worked 32 hours per week, took numerous babysitting jobs, and still made excellent grades with a full academic load. I was thrilled when she quickly demonstrated a flair for writing and decided to major in journalism when she transferred to Texas A&M. As for Beth Ann, she returned to her postgraduate studies and graduate assistantship, also at Texas A&M. Meanwhile, Gail continued to earn accolades from parents and teachers alike.

Having finally resigned myself that I would never get ahead at the FDIC, I took solace in the fact that I was working with some wonderful colleagues. Eventually, I was given responsibility for marketing all the "unmarketable assets." Doing this meant fixing any problem, or more often, problems that had landed each property in the boneyard called "unmarketable." The ultimate goal for each piece of real estate that the FDIC acquired was to turn it into cash—those that could not because they were contaminated or otherwise unsellable were considered unmarketable. We managed to find solutions so all the properties became marketable and saleable.

Despite hitting a wall, I threw myself into my work, and enjoyed it. I was naive enough to believe that doing great work would assure me a place at the FDIC for as long as I wanted to work. In 2004, I began looking for the exit when the new FDIC chairman, a lifelong banker, visited the Dallas office. When he announced that our first responsibility was "not to inconvenience open banks," I immediately looked at my colleague to my left and found him grimacing and turned to my right in time to catch a similar expression. I had seen enough by then to consider a buyout offer in early 2005. Once again, I saw the hand of the Lord: I met the tenure requirement by just two months.

By then both of my daughters had graduated from college and gotten married. Beth Ann had begun working on her Ph.D. in special education, while teaching elementary school. Gail and I couldn't help but feel an extra sense of satisfaction in Beth Ann's pursuit of an advanced degree. We found satisfaction in the fact that Beth Ann scored in the top 10 percent of her peers on the GRE—the same exam that had bedeviled the gifted and talented coordinator so many years earlier, preventing her from being accepted into the Texas Tech Ph.D. program. Of course, Gail and I were not surprised, since

Beth Ann had been inducted into both the National Honor Society and the National Math Honor Society in high school. She had also been inducted into the honors track at A&M at the end of her freshman year and later graduated cum laude.

Gail was offered an opportunity to retire with the promise of immediately being rehired. This meant she could draw full retirement and full pay at the same time; needless to say, she jumped at the chance. This arrangement, though the exception, was sometimes used to encourage teachers of subjects where teacher shortages existed to remain in the profession longer than they otherwise might. The incentive was used to encourage exceptionally skilled teachers, like Gail, to extend their careers.

CHAPTER 19

MOVING ON

I wasn't exactly pushing my way to the front of the line to take the FDIC's buyout offer. By this time, I was earning in the six figures, and able to make a sizable retirement contribution each year. If I left, the FDIC would pay me a bonus of about half my yearly salary. If I declined the buyout and subsequently lost my job, there would be no buyout. On the other hand, if I did not accept the buyout and kept my job, over the next seven years, my total earnings would be close to seven figures by the time I would qualify for full Social Security benefits. Plus, my retirement nest egg would have grown by about an additional $300,000. I had come a long way from my childhood—and had clearly proved all the naysayers wrong.

We were informed that all military veterans would be able to retain their positions regardless of their individual work histories. This mandate, along with the mandate to hire and promote more women, made me feel like I was being discriminated against—albeit legally. While I certainly agree that veterans are due our utmost respect and gratitude, there was an obvious disconnect for me. Because of my sight impairment, I had never been afforded the option of serving in the armed services, thus never had the opportunity to "earn" this preferential treatment.

Even more disconcerting was the revelation that annual performance evaluations and similar measures of work performance would not be considered at all in deciding who would be retained—I never knew why. This was the point at which I finally realized how naive I had been in believing hard work and a history of exceptional performance reviews would assure me a future with the FDIC. The fact of the matter was that no one at the FDIC had much control over what was going on—that was the domain of the Office of Personnel Management (OPM) in Washington, D.C. The OPM made the final decision regarding who would stay and who would go. It was ironic: I had been officially recognized for my contributions, and now the ability to keep that job was being threatened by the same organization (the federal government). Arbitrary actions that violated reason and fair play had always incensed me, and this most recent experience was no exception. I was so repelled by what I observed that I began searching for a new career in earnest, a career where merit would be how I was judged.

Because we were given several months to decide whether we wanted to accept the buyout, I decided to make full use of the advanced warning. During that time, the FDIC provided career counselors to coach us, and I attended every seminar, sought individual assistance, and learned how to prepare a résumé that does not give away my age—all the while showcasing my achievements and skills.

The counselors encouraged us to look for a career doing something that we might have considered a hobby in the past—something that was a personal interest and more than just a job. For me, that meant writing, public speaking, teaching, working with numbers, doing long-range planning, and conducting research—especially research into economic and stock market patterns. Over the next several months, I painstakingly prepared résumés tailored to specific positions and submitted them. As had happened in the past, I received no responses. None.

I considered teaching college students. My two master's degrees would help at the community college level, but I would need a Ph.D. to teach at a four-year institution. I was certainly willing to earn a Ph.D. while working as an instructor and explored several possible positions, including at Texas A&M.

Undaunted by the enormous pay cut I would have to accept if I wanted to transition into academia, I met with the head of the urban planning department. His response? "Why on earth would you want to do this?" He went on to share that he typically worked 80 hours per week and devoted 80 percent of his time to research and writing, leaving him little time for actual teaching. That was all I needed to know to decide that this would have been a bad decision. Working 80 hours per week did not scare me, because I expected to do that at least until completing a Ph.D. The reduced salary didn't scare me.

What scared me was the prospect of giving students nothing but the leftovers of my time and energy. In this case, if I couldn't, I decided it was better not to give at all.

While I wanted to work another 25 to 30 years, it became increasingly clear that age discrimination was a fact of life for people over 50, even more so for those approaching 60. Like most prejudices, the underlying assumption is the exact opposite of the truth. Older employees are likely to be more committed to their organization, and despite the stereotypes, are open to learning, including new technologies. About this time—2004—a lawsuit was filed against the FDIC (65 FLRA No. 63). This case alleged discrimination by the FDIC in its allocation of rewards, in which African-Americans and persons over the age of 50 received unfair treatment. The matter was finally arbitrated in 2010 with the FDIC paying $2.61 million to impacted parties. In 2004 and 2005, the rumor mill at the FDIC had it that a tape recording had surfaced in which high-level FDIC officials had discussed methods for purging the organization of its older employees. I am not sure there was any truth to the rumors, but it was easy to believe for those of us over age 50 who were considering the buyout, especially after having sent out many résumés without receiving the courtesy of a single acknowledgment. The filing of a lawsuit alleging age discrimination suggested to me and others that the FDIC's senior management bought into the many prejudices against older workers. Whether the assessment I and others made at the time was fair or not is less clear after the 2010 arbitrated settlement. For many of us older workers, the message seemed clear: younger and cheaper is better than older, more knowledgeable, and perhaps more loyal. There was, however, another financial consideration: those who had completed 20 years of qualified federal service and were at least 55 years old would be eligible to receive a pension and a Social Security stipend—if they accepted the FDIC's offer. The stipend would help bridge any gap between a retiree's age at accepting the offer and when Social Security retirement benefits commenced. To sweeten the deal further, the FDIC offered to pay 80 percent of the cost of health care insurance for life and to provide the equivalent of one year's salary in life insurance until age 65 and one-fourth that amount until death after age 65.

When I did the math, I calculated that I would squeak by with 20 years and two months of service. Having spent months thinking and praying about what I should do, I considered my slim margin of eligibility a matter of God's providence—I accepted the deal. I knew that I wanted to work for as long as I could. However, the prospect of commuting from Carrollton to downtown Dallas every day for an additional 20–30 years did not appeal to me. Getting up every morning at 5:15 in order to make my 90-minute commute work was getting old. But most important was that the sense of purpose I had felt earlier working at the FDIC was long gone. It was time to move on.

Finally, after agonizing for months, my decision was made. I called Nancy Ray, a classmate from high school I had become reacquainted with. While Nancy and I scarcely knew each other in school, we had developed a friendship when attending class reunions. Nancy had been a financial advisor for a dozen years, and I told her I was considering becoming a financial advisor because it played into many of my personal interests. I asked her if she thought I had lost my mind. "Not at all," and added that she thought I would be outstanding. While I was sure the decades of economic and stock market analysis experience I had could help me provide good investment advice, I was not sure it was the higher-calling I sought at this point in my life.

When I finally left the FDIC, I still didn't know what the future held for me. I did know, however, that I was happy to be moving on.

CHAPTER 20

FUTURE FORWARD

At the time I left the FDIC, I had also been teaching for the Hadley School for the Blind for about five years. Based in Winnetka, Illinois, the Hadley School is the world's largest school for the blind. When I began teaching there in 2000, more than 10,000 students from more than 90 countries were taking courses, all of which were provided remotely and free of charge. In fact, the campus at Winnetka has no classrooms. The school offered a wide range of programs, including a curriculum leading to a high school diploma and a host of continuing education courses. Lessons are submitted in a variety of formats including Braille, type, handwritten, audio, and e-mail. Roughly 80 percent of the school's students have some usable sight, a characteristic that mirrors the larger blind population, including me.

Despite its size and fame, I had never heard of the school until I received a call from their dean of education. She told me she was trying to find an instructor for two business courses and that I had been recommended.

Because the school had employees with a wide range of visual acuity, from fully-sighted, sight-impaired, to totally blind, I assimilated seamlessly. Students submitted their lessons directly to the school, and those lessons were then forwarded to me. Because I did not read Braille, lessons submitted in that format were translated before being delivered to me. Once graded, I mailed each lesson to the student in an envelope bearing the school's return address.

I taught personal financial planning, and small business management— students had a wide range of backgrounds, ages, and aspirations, but most were trying to equip themselves to find a job. A fraction of my students were college educated; a few were brilliant. Others had very little formal education and struggled with English. Some lived in large cities, while others were in obscure third-world villages. Occasionally, a student would report a delay in recording his lessons because there was no electricity in his village. Despite their many differences, all of my students shared a desire to learn and a struggle against a merciless condition. I loved every one of them even though I never saw any of their faces, and I strove to enrich each of their lives. These values were not unique to me; they were apparent in every Hadley associate I ever met. Needless to say, this was a fulfilling part of my life.

Typically, I spent about 20 hours per week teaching and grading papers. Once I left the FDIC, this schedule allowed me to focus on applying for full-time positions that interested me.

During this time, I took charge of our investments in a way not possible while at the FDIC. As is typically the case with employer-sponsored plans such as 401(k) and 403(b), my investment choices were limited to a small number of mutual funds. The more than 30 years I had devoted to studying economic and stock market patterns finally produced big dividends. Once I parted ways with the FDIC, I was able to roll my 401(k) into an Individual Retirement Account (IRA), which meant I was no longer limited to a small number of mutual funds. Having embraced what I called "a get rich slow" approach, I was surprised by the results. There was certainly more at work here than me making good investment choices: the stock, bond, and commodity markets were all cooperating. Even so, the knowledge to recognize what was "on sale" made a big difference and enabled me to make some smart choices. Actively managing our investments was like having a new job, and it prepared me for the road ahead—although I didn't know it at the time. More importantly, I loved it.

As I continued my search for a new career, I had certain goals in mind. In addition to wanting to put my education to use, I wanted to help others. Caring for Janie, and coping with my own struggles, had helped me develop far more empathy and caring than might otherwise have been the case. I was fortunate to be in a position where earning a large salary did not have to be a priority—Gail and I were empty nesters and had sufficient retirement savings. What I wanted most of all was intellectually challenging work that took advantage of my skills and energy.

About this time, the position of president of the Hadley School became available, and I applied for it. Admittedly, my resume was not a perfect match.

My vision for the school meant taking it down a different path. I envisioned a university with blind and sight-impaired persons as its focus but one open to sighted students as well. Based on my own experience, I believe that blind and sight-impaired individuals as a group can be far more adept at forming hypotheses than their fully sighted counterparts because we are forced to use very limited information to hypothesize about our environments. My goal was to create an institution of sight-impaired individuals who could produce an extraordinary think tank that could benefit science, government, and business. Having attended five colleges and universities without ever once encountering another severely sight-impaired person, I would like to see students like me have a radically different choice—and experience—in education.

I felt that my skills in long-range planning, banking, and business management could provide an alternative to a more traditional background. Neither Gail nor I wanted to move to Illinois, but we agreed we would if the school's board embraced my radical vision—they did not. The experience was one I certainly don't regret; in fact, it empowered me, and allowed me to take risks that I may not have otherwise. It also reflected the effort I was willing to expend to find God's gig for me—turns out God had bigger plans in mind for me than I did.

I continued to explore other areas of interest, including developing courses in church long-range planning, and becoming a full-time writer and author. Neither idea went anywhere. I was once again drawn toward becoming a financial advisor. I thought a great deal about my earlier conversation with Nancy. One of my concerns was feeling pressured to push products that were not a perfect fit for a client's needs. She assured me that I would never feel pressured to sell anything I did not believe was in the best interests of my clients: "It will never happen." She had also told me about the many families who had reached their financial goals thanks to her work with them—including sending kids to college and meeting retirement goals. She also talked about how many close personal friends she had made as an advisor. I had a sort of epiphany: as a financial planner, I could be in the *stress reduction* business. At last, I knew what I wanted to do, perhaps for the rest of my life. My decision was made.

Getting where I am today has involved a lot of long hours and hard work—but I was ready. The organization I work in has a culture in which experienced professionals give their time to help the new hires—sometimes even before they get hired. Even more important, there were no needless barriers. I was 60 years old and legally blind when I was hired, and it was never an issue. If an individual is intelligent, has integrity, the right interpersonal skills, and is willing to work hard, the organization will support them. I am testament to that.

My new position meant taking many initiatives, and these were generally more difficult for me because of my sight impairment. To give you an idea, as part of the application process, you are required to knock on the doors of strangers until you have completed 25 interviews. Before doing this, I explained to appropriate individuals in our home office some of the obstacles I would face because of my sight impairment: I couldn't drive around the area to be canvassed, and in most cases I would not even be able to see the house number (necessary to complete the standardized form required). On certain surfaces, I would have trouble seeing steps or even slight changes in elevations—a problem exacerbated by changes in shadows, glare, and the presence of household and playground items on the walkway. In some cases, I would not be able to find the button for the doorbell. The biggest obstacle would be when someone answered the door: would I be able to determine if the person was the head of household or a minor? I needed to either read or memorize all the questions and somehow record the responses correctly—and legibly. These challenges were all in addition to the typical challenges someone would face while going through the job application process.

To address these concerns, I limited my canvassing to our neighborhood so I wouldn't have to worry about driving. Next, I got a clipboard and produced a couple dozen copies of the standardized form in a huge font, and secured a giant felt-tipped marker. By staying in the neighborhood where Gail and I had walked many times, the terrain was flat, and the entryways were already familiar. I could pretty much avoid stumbling, falling or careening. Using markers on the exaggerated forms and holding my face near the clipboard to write made it obvious that I was severely sight-impaired. I didn't hesitate to let people know I was legally blind. When I could sense that people felt uncomfortable, I would lighten the mood by saying to them, "Don't forget my motto." Almost always, the question would come back, "What is your motto?" To this I would say, "Don't wave." With few exceptions, this would produce a laugh and break the ice. In one instance, I came upon a couple coming out of their house about to get into their car. I introduced myself and inquired about their occupations. The man said he was an air traffic controller at Dallas-Fort Worth airport. I put my gigantic marker down, moved my face away from the clipboard, looked right at him and asked if they had any job openings I might pursue. Shaking his head and laughing, he responded, "Maybe not." With that they quickly got in the car and left. He never became a client, but I did achieve my goal to make myself unforgettable—in a favorable way.

After going through a few more hoops, I received an offer. One condition of the offer was the requirement that I give up all part-time employment to ensure I was focused. By then, the Hadley School had gone in a direction that I didn't agree with, so it was an easy decision.

As a new employee, getting the computer logistics ironed out proved a lengthy and frustrating challenge for me—and for the firm. There were numerous incompatibilities between the company's proprietary software applications and the visual enhancement software available for use with more common products such as Microsoft Word and Excel. Working frequently with the home office, we looked for work-arounds and stopgap measures—real fixes came much more slowly.

The first problem we encountered arose when a computer laptop arrived at my home. A totally blind technician had loaded his favorite adaptive software onto the laptop. While the program (Jaws) is widely embraced by the totally blind community, it doesn't work well for someone with partial sight. Eager to be helpful, the tech who was helping me with setup told me not to worry because there was an app that enlarged print. Unfortunately, it was not designed for severely sight-impaired people. Besides providing inferior visual images, it did not read the text aloud. I needed to use the laptop to study for the Series 7 Exam, required if I wanted to be a financial advisor and sell securities. I suggested the study material simply be e-mailed to my personal computer, so I could both see it and have it read to me. After each chapter, I would call in and arrange for someone to test me over the material. This process was time-consuming, but the training department agreed. We were all convinced I would pass the exam on the first try.

Only the bar and CPA exams are more difficult than the Series 7. Before taking the bar exam, candidates invest three years in law school, and many

CPA candidates work as bookkeepers and tax preparers for years prior to sitting for the exam. By contrast, those who aspire to become financial advisors typically study for a month or two on a full-time basis or part-time for up to a year. The Series 7, like most examinations for professional certifications, is administered under the strictest protocol by official testing firms. Every possible safeguard is taken to prevent cheating and to ensure that each person taking the exam receives exactly the same treatment.

To assist those who are severely sight-impaired, the testing agency arranges for human readers. Because using a third party to read the material aloud and to reread passages on an as-needed basis takes longer, twice the normal testing time is allotted. Typically, the Series 7 is administered in two three-hour increments, one in the morning and the other in the afternoon, plus a one-hour break for lunch. Limited breaks in the morning and afternoon sessions were also allowed under strict guidelines. To double the testing time means providing 12 hours plus a break. To find a testing center that was open 13 consecutive hours, I had to travel to Austin from our home in Carrollton— about 200 miles. This meant postponing my exam for an additional month, traveling to Austin one day, and taking the exam the next. The personnel folks worked closely with officials of the testing agency to ensure that everything would come off without a hitch; they involved me in the conversations so everyone understood what would transpire.

Two human readers would be provided in two shifts. I was assured that I would receive up to twice the normal testing time. While the testing agency would not permit me to use visual enhancement software on their computer so I could see the computer screen, I would be allowed to bring my magnifier/ reader (CCTV), and follow along with the human reader using a print copy.

On the Friday before Labor Day, 2006, I entered the testing center in Austin, carrying my CCTV. As I entered the door, I was told that I would not be allowed to see a print copy of the exam, as promised. At that moment, I could feel my blood pressure rising, which caused a huge opacity to appear across the surface of my dominant eye. This meant I could scarcely see enough to continue walking while carrying my machine. Over the more than 55 years I had been dealing with limited sight, I had experienced similar opacities only a few times. It was scary, but I knew the problem would dissipate within about 20 minutes. Amazingly, I never felt overwhelmed because my self-confidence kicked in—plus I knew that this was the Lord's plan for me. I never questioned my knowledge of the subject matter nor the quality of instruction I had gotten from the firm. I never questioned my ability to analyze every word of every question and apply what I had learned. My greatest source of inner strength came from a lifetime of confronting threats and threatening circumstances—sooner or later, I came out ahead.

After placing my machine on a table in the examination room, I was led out to an area where I was to empty my pockets, remove my watch from my arm, and the ball point pen from my shirt pocket. I was given two sheets of paper along with two pencils and told I could use my viewer to make notes to myself throughout the test.

My first reader introduced himself, started the computer, and began reading the introductory messages. One of those messages announced that the program would close down after three hours, at which time the morning session would end. Immediately, I summoned a testing official who assured me not to worry. Before long, I had nailed the first dozen or so questions without a second thought—any apprehension I had was now gone. A few minutes before noon, I completed the morning session. As I left for lunch, I was pleased with myself for having completed the session within the standard time frame and was confident I had passed. After lunch, the same reader returned and announced he would work for a couple more hours before being replaced. Once again, he started the computer and read aloud the introductory messages. Once again, there was a warning that the system would shut off after three hours. Once again, I was told not to worry.

The afternoon session progressed more slowly because there were numerous questions requiring the use of a handheld calculator. Using the calculator while holding it under the camera mounted in my viewer was awkward, time-consuming, and tiring. After about an hour into the afternoon session, my second reader took over. I had declined to take a break during the morning session, but because of the slower pace that promised to make the afternoon session longer, about an hour into the second reader's shift I decided to take a break to down a candy bar and soft drink. About 15 minutes after I returned, the computer flashed a message that it was terminating the exam immediately, and shut down. I was shocked, angry, and now a bit panic-stricken, though I managed to keep my cool. I began firing questions at testing officials, aimed at finding a suitable solution. I asked the resident tech if he could add the additional time—neither he nor anyone in the organization's office could. I asked if I could retake the afternoon session only if I passed the earlier one. No one knew the answer. I asked whether I would be given a pass if I had earned enough points at the time the machine shut down. No one knew the answer to that question either. I was told that my questions would have to be answered by the testing firm's home office, and they were closed until the following Tuesday. Ordinarily, test takers find out immediately after completing the exam whether they passed or not. I now had to wait three days, which meant a long, unsettling weekend. On Tuesday morning, I learned I had earned 78 points before the machine had shut down. Fortunately, only 70 points are needed to pass. One exam down, one to go!

Next up was studying for and passing the Series 66 exam. The study materials for this exam were not available in electronic form, so I could not use my computer to read the material. Gail rescued me, as she often did. We didn't have enough time for her to read all the text, so I picked select passages and tried to absorb as much as possible. This time I was able to go to a testing center much closer to home. Once again, I had a human reader. This time, I finished the whole test on time and scored 81. I was on my way.

Like all beginning advisors, I was required to prospect for clients. This meant knocking on 4,000–5,000 doors in my territory, while encountering all the obstacles I had confronted when conducting the initial canvas of 25 homes. I would have to spend at least 1,000 hours knocking on doors, and before I could begin, I needed to choose a territory. My 10 years as a city planner was a huge help here. I knew I wanted to relocate to the northern fringe of the Dallas North expansion that had been going on for 100 years or longer. Specifically, I wanted to locate in one of the larger, rapidly growing cities, McKinney. Gail and I checked out a couple of prospective locations identified by the home office team and began to look for a place to live. We decided to build a new home in a subdivision about a mile from the future office site. The area featured lighted walking and bike trails under all its thoroughfares, which meant I could walk to work without crossing any major streets.

I still needed to meet a requirement to introduce myself to approximately 1,000 people. The first major milestone toward this goal was 400 households. Once I reached that level, I qualified to attend a week of training at the firm's headquarters. To give you an idea of the support I received by this organization, I arrived early so I could meet with two IT technicians. They needed to work on a laptop to try and solve the content incompatibility issues that had been plaguing me for months. These folks were willing to give up their Sunday to help me. Additionally, a CCTV and a visually enhanced computer were available to me by Monday morning when the training started.

About this time, I was offered an opportunity to share an office with Dick and Lori Stevens, a rare financial advisor and Branch Office Administrator (BOA) husband and wife team. Lori has probably contributed more to my success as an advisor than anyone else—she was always accessible, intelligent, calm, and helpful. While at Dick's and Lori's office, I received my broker's license. By the following June, in 2007, I had received three awards, including the Pioneer Award for first-year financial advisors who opened at least 120 new accounts.

A few months later, God smiled on me again. As I was just about to meet the requirement to get my own branch office, I got a call from another financial advisor who had just trained a BOA that now needed a job. I interviewed Bobbie in my home, and immediately knew we would make a great team.

A few months later, Bobbie and I moved to our new office. Working with Bobbie and having my own office was a milestone for me. I felt as if I had finally completed boot camp and gotten my commission. The most unpleasant part of my new career was behind me, and I spent the next six years working six days a week, with few exceptions. This wasn't expected of me—it was just part of my DNA.

All good things must come to an end, and for family reasons, Bobbie took a position closer to her home. I ended up hiring Deb Taylor, a woman I knew from the Chamber of Commerce. If having a good BOA is integral to the success of the typical financial advisor, it is absolutely crucial to mine because of my sight impairment.

We have about 250 households that look to us to reduce their stress. Deb and I have formed a bond with most of these clients. My new career brings together all the goals I have had throughout my working life: teaching, calming, encouraging, and reasoning. God truly has smiled on me.

EPILOGUE
BLESSED

While it would be wonderful to enjoy normal vision, the big picture for me is very, very bright. At the end of the day, life is hard—even for the most fortunate of us. Certainly, I have had my share of hardships as well as blessings. Among my greatest heartaches has been the vision loss of my girls—most notably Beth Ann—and more recently of our grandson, Garrett. Like his mother, Garrett's vision was quite good during his toddler years and then deteriorated to a level apparently worse than his mother's. Like every parent or grandparent who passes along an insidious ingredient in the gene pool, I feel a deep pain. Even so, there is every reason to expect that Garrett will achieve great things in his life and experience the joy that I, and his mother, have known. Not only are Garrett's mother and I uniquely equipped to help him, his father illustrates the same kind of judgment in working with Garrett on the family farm as my father used towards me in his plumbing business.

The attitudes and accommodations afforded Beth Ann have been far greater than those I knew. And the attitudes and accommodations Garrett will encounter will be more favorable still. We will do what high-functioning families do everywhere: take the future together and with a legacy of overcoming obstacles. For even when impaired, we are richly empowered.

. . .

Several factors motivated me to write this book. As I mentioned earlier in this book, I have aspired to become a sculptor of elegant and compelling thoughts, both as a writer and as a speaker. Just as a young musician strives for years to refine his craft to produce pleasure for others as well as himself, so it has been with me.

I have shared my story—even the parts that were hard to share—with the hope that other individuals with impairments will be encouraged and given practical insights. In particular, I want to equip family members, educators, pastors, and friends of children with disabilities to be skilled facilitators. The following principles surfaced throughout this book, and are directed to parents, guardians, or professionals seeking to assist a child who possesses a disability. In an effort to minimize awkward phrasing, I have chosen this format realizing that many of my readers are mature disabled individuals, fully capable of advocating for themselves. The unmistakable theme of these remarks is the importance of believing and trusting:

- Believe in the intelligence of your child. By intelligence, I mean the ability to accomplish tasks. Thought of in this way, almost everyone can be successful. I.Q. is a much narrower definition of intelligence and was conceived to predict the ability of children to perform in grammar school, a job it has performed without great distinction. Dr. Austin Kerley of Texas A&M University said, "I suspect more children have been hurt by I.Q. tests than have been helped by them." I am convinced that is even more true when it comes to sensory-impaired youngsters such as the sight- or hearing-impaired. If one or more standardized tests indicate that your child is bright, you can be sure they are. Unfortunately, if such instruments suggest a lower ability level, believe in yourself. When a child's teacher and a parent believe standardized tests provide a false reading, I would side with the parent and teacher every time. I do not believe for one minute that intelligence is fixed for life. Sensory-impaired persons spend virtually every waking minute solving problems. They are constantly forming hypotheses about what they are hearing or seeing and searching for the most appropriate response. How could that possibly help but build mental functioning? The great danger in tagging a youngster with an intelligence rating that is too low is that it will become a self-fulfilling prophecy. Parents and teachers often lower expectations for a child based on standardized tests. Do not, under any circumstances, allow this to happen to your child.
- Believe in others. Encourage your child to operate from a position of strength when seeking to develop relationships. Teach your child to have self-esteem by striving to be the best possible person. Explain that

time spent trying to minimize the appearance of one's impairment in the eyes of another is generally time wasted. Instead, help them to focus on the reasons why they admire another person and seek friendship or a romantic relationship with them. Teach your child that most people respond very favorably when others express admiration for them. Instill the truth that conversation is the best tool for developing relationships. There will always be naive people out there who might make an inappropriate response, but that just exposes their weaknesses. Teach your child to believe that most people recognize and respect character.

- Believe in asking for help: Many people, especially those who have chosen people-centered careers, realize the joy that comes from helping someone else. Parents, educators, pastors, counselors, and case workers have all signed up to be inconvenienced by someone just like you. Most have given up a more lucrative career to help others. Let them do their jobs. Help your child know the difference between seeking someone to do his work for him, and seeking someone to help him do the parts he cannot do alone.

- Believe in technology: Take your child to visit a center where adaptive equipment is on display. Engage persons at such a center to describe how technology has advanced over the years. Encourage your child to imagine a technological advancement that would make her life better and then help her believe such a breakthrough is possible.

- Believe in planning. Teach your child to set goals and strategies for meeting those goals. Use these goals and strategies to achieve bite-sized objectives as a means for illustrating the value of hard work and careful thinking.

- Believe the future can be much better than the present. Show your child how rewarding it can be to control much about your own destiny.

- Believe in God. Every mature person possessing normal mental faculties has no choice but to live by faith. There are those voices in our society that would have us believe that traditional religious views are only embraced by those outside the intellectual elite—people who lack sophistication. Don't believe it, and don't let your child believe it. My walk by faith, while certainly less than perfect, has allowed me to observe firsthand, "The substance of things hoped for and the evidence of things not seen." Hebrews 11.

AFTERWORD

As you read my father's story, you no doubt realized there was a total absence of special education service through his educational journey. In addition to the lack of services, Dad did not enjoy the use of assistive technology to facilitate his participation. In fact, it was not until he was working on his master's degree that he secured the use of a tape recorder so he could tape lectures. He often had to have readers read the first and last paragraphs of chapter sections, as he did not have any other way to access his textbooks or the time to read the entirety of course materials.

Thankfully, things have changed since then. As a legally blind person, although I still experienced biases, especially with regard to formal evaluation procedures, my educational experience was much more positive. After my diagnosis in 1984, I received accommodations and the support of a low vision coordinator. Although there was a lot more in the way of technology available to me than to Dad, I did not utilize it until I was working on my dissertation. Perhaps if this had been a skill specifically taught to me, I would have used it to a greater extent. My underutilization of available technology was likely exacerbated by the fact that I, much like Dad had felt in comparison to Janie, did not feel like the disabled one in our family—I always told people of my dad who is legally blind while pretending I fit in among the totally sighted. I always knew in the back of my mind that my vision was different, but, after all, I didn't know anyone my age with vision difficulties and this was the only vision I had ever known.

My son, Garrett, who is embarking on his educational voyage in the second decade of the 21st century, is already benefiting from the services of a low vision itinerant teacher, orientation and mobility considerations, and occupational therapy. He has, from kindergarten, been exposed to a CCTV and hand-held video magnifier, both with rotatable cameras (allowing both near and far vision), a scope for distance, and portable magnifiers. Garrett has attended his own individual education program (IEP) meetings to practice advocating for himself and is working on telling his teacher, without prompting, when he cannot see something in his environment. Perhaps most importantly, Garrett has already been involved in events for students with visual impairments—events where he is exposed to others with similar visual acuity. He has been able to learn from an early age that he is not the only one in the world dealing with the struggles associated with vision loss—this can go a long way to remediating feelings of loneliness and isolation.

The trends noted here are indicative of the promising horizons for special education and treatment of individuals with disabilities. In addition to improved community access, educational services for individuals with disabilities have improved leaps and bounds in the last fifty years, and it has been this response to the needs of students with disabilities that has made a difference in their lives and in their outcomes.[1]

As is often the case, it has taken the intercession of the courts to prompt social justice for individuals with disabilities, as litigation, in turn, prompted legislative action. Even though it took time, the landmark civil rights case, *Brown v. Board of Education* (1954), which found the practice of separating children due to race was not equal, provided the basis for future rulings involving educating students with disabilities—namely, that children with disabilities can no longer be excluded from school and are entitled to a free and appropriate education.[2,3] It was sixteen years later when two federal district court cases, *Pennsylvania Association for Retarded Children (PARC) v. Commonwealth of Pennsylvania* (1972) and *Mills v. Board of Education of the District of Columbia* (1972), applied the equal opportunity concept to students with disabilities. While there had been other legislative actions aimed at education, these two cases laid the groundwork for legislative response for students with disabilities. In 1975, the Education of All Handicapped Children Act (EAHCA) was born. The EAHCA, or P.L. 94–142, established the educational rights of students with disabilities (i.e., to be included in school with non-disabled peers, with programming appropriate for their needs) and federal funding to the states to facilitate

---

1 Fuchs, D. & Young, C. L. (2006). "On the irrelevance of intelligence in predicting responsiveness to reading instruction." *Exceptional Children, 73*, 8–30.

2 Smith, D. & Tyler, N. (2010). *Introduction to Special Education* (6th ed.). Upper Saddle River, N.J.: Pearson Education, Inc.

3 Yell, M. (2012). *The Law and Special Education* (3rd ed.). Upper Saddle River, N.J.: Pearson Education, Inc.

compliance—assuming states submitted plans for meeting the new requirements. By 1985, all states had met the requirements of EAHCA and EAHCA has been reauthorized four times to expand and better define services for students with disabilities; it is now known as the Individuals with Disabilities Education Act (IDEA).[4]

The Individuals with Disabilities Education Act guarantees certain educational rights for individuals with disabilities. First, the Act mandates nondiscriminatory testing procedures be utilized in the identification of students with disabilities; thus, the results of one test cannot be used as the sole basis for admission into special education. Once students are deemed eligible for special education services, the Act establishes that they are entitled to a free and appropriate education (FAPE) provided in the least restrictive environment (LRE). This means that students should be educated, at no cost to their families, with nondisabled peers to the maximum extent appropriate. To facilitate the provision of FAPE and placement in the LRE, the Act requires that all students with disabilities have an IEP drafted to meet their individual needs. The Act also sets a standard that no student should be turned away from an education, or a zero-reject policy, and that parents have a right to participate in the education of their children. Finally, the Act establishes a system of checks and balances, or due process and procedural safeguards, to ensure parental rights and a process for dispute resolution.[5]

It was with calculated purpose that Congress included parents in IDEA—to help make sure that students with disabilities received appropriate services: the importance of parental involvement in education is well-documented. Parents completing homework with their children, attending school functions, and communicating/collaborating with school personnel are all factors that directly impact student achievement.[6] Increased parental involvement is also associated with decreased high school dropout[7] and higher educational

---

4   Ibid.

5   Individuals with Disabilities Education Act. (2004). [34 CFR 300.307] [20 U.S.C. 1221e-3; 1401(30); 1414(b)(6)] Retrieved from http://idea.ed.gov/explore/view/p/%2 Croot%2Cdynamic%2CTopicalBrief%2C23%2C

6   Jeynes, W. H. (2007). "The relationship between parent involvement and urban secondary school student academic achievement." *Urban Education, 42*, 82–110.

7   Barnard, W. M. (2003). "Parent involvement in elementary school and educational attainment." *Children and Youth Services Review, 26*, 39–62.

expectations,[8] improved school attendance,[9] and decreased at-risk behavior.[10] Alternatively, "[a] lack of parental participation leads to inappropriate and unsound educational programs for students with disabilities."[11]

A few of the procedures that IDEA delineates to foster parental participation include parental consent for evaluations, parental notice of IEP meetings, and established procedural safeguards.[12] The knowledge of established legal protections and the impact of parental involvement on student achievement can only serve to empower parents to exercise their rights to the fullest extent of the law. It is because of advocates that paved the way before us that individuals with disabilities enjoy much improved services and access today.[13] I consider my father one of those advocates. Students with disabilities will continue to require advocacy—largely on the part of their parents. It is absolutely crucial, then, that parents become familiar with special education procedures and processes and learn to "speak the language" of special education. This can be accomplished in many ways: joining support groups for parents of students with disabilities, attending professional development seminars and professional conferences, and employing the services of a hired advocate/legal representative to attend school meetings and provide guidance.[14,15]

As our family has demonstrated—especially my father—we may be impaired but we are empowered.

—Beth A. Ashby Jones, Ph.D.

8   Jeynes

9   Epstein, J. L. & Sheldon, S. B. (2002). "Present and accounted for: Improving student attendance through family and community involvement." *Journal of Educational Research, 95*, 308–318.

10 Vakalahi, H. F. (2001). "Adolescent substance abuse and family-based risk and protective factors: A literature review." *Journal of Drug Education, 31*, 29–46.

11 Fish, W. W. (2008). "The IEP meeting: Perceptions of parents of students who receive special education services." *Preventing School Failure, 53*, 8–14.

12 Individuals with Disabilities Act.

13 Yell

14 Bacon, J. & Causton-Theoharis, J. (2013). "'It should be teamwork': a critical investigation of school practices and parent advocacy in special education." *International Journal of Inclusive Education, 17*(7), 682–699.

15 Burke, M. (2015). "Improving parental involvement: Training special education advocates." *Journal of Disability Policy Studies, 23*(4), 225–234.

ACKNOWLEDGMENTS

Impaired, But Empowered has been a work-in-progress since 1968—that's when I first realized how totally misinformed most people were about what it means to be legally blind. The ignorance of many otherwise brilliant individuals simply stunned me. Unbeknownst to me at the time, I would need another half-century or so of life experiences to produce a work that addresses two major goals: 1) Encourages persons with physical and learning impairments to set and attain stretch goals for themselves; and 2) Helps the broader public to think more accurately and constructively about disabled individuals. Along the way, the following individuals contributed significantly to the writing process:

My wife, Gail, to whom this book is dedicated, helped me search for common characteristics among 100 best-selling books before I started writing.

Maryann Young, a successful author of historical novels, got me started and reviewed early drafts.

Emma Vandaventer, retired English teacher, tutored me in grammar and style.

Doug Woodward, professional colleague and personal friend, reviewed and provided feedback on a very early draft.

Barbara Brock, retired language arts teacher, discovered a few late-stage typos.

Dr. Beth Jones, Assistant Professor of Special Education, Texas A&M Commerce, reviewed the manuscript, provided feedback, and contributed the afterword.

Heidi Jordan, family friend, reviewed and provided feedback on the entire manuscript.

David Wilkinson, editor of "Baptist News Global," read the draft and made valuable stylistic recommendations.

Carolyn Corbin, author and retired international speaker, read the manuscript and recommended an outstanding literary agent.

Cynthia Zigmund, literary agent, Second City Publishing, helped me more than I could ever say make the transition from technical writer to story teller.

Dr. Daniel Vestal, Distinguished University Professor of Baptist Leadership and Director of the Eula Mae and John Baugh Center for Baptist Leadership at Mercer University, read the manuscript and provided feedback.

Billy Brookshire, lifelong friend, author, and tireless advocate for the visually impaired through his work at the Texas Commission for the Blind, read the manuscript and contributed the foreword.

ABOUT THE AUTHOR

When Walter D. Ashby was a boy, doctors told his parents not to expect much: he wouldn't graduate from high school, let alone attend college. He would never drive, and probably wouldn't do anything meaningful with his life. Walter suffered from a rare genetic disorder—optic atrophy—that left him legally blind. Instead of accepting his disability as an impediment, Walter viewed it as a challenge. By relying on faith—along with his own initiative and a handful of caring adults, including his father—not only did he graduate from high school and college (with a B.A. in History and Government from Tarleton State University), Walter earned two graduate degrees (Master's of Urban and Regional Planning from Texas A&M University, and an MBA from the University of Texas of the Permian Basin). He married the girl of his dreams, became a father, and has enjoyed a long and successful professional career.

Walter is a top financial advisor with Edward Jones. Prior to joining the firm, he prospered as a director of urban planning, a senior city planner, an adjunct professor, and as a director of marketing research, and held several positions within the FDIC. He also is an accomplished business writer. While all of these positions represented a challenge because of his disability, Walter thrived thanks to his faith and fortitude. For his achievements and courage, Walter was selected to receive the 1990 Presidential Award for Most Outstanding Federal Employees with Disabilities.

Walter is a big believer in giving back to his community—he served as president for both the Midland (Texas) Special Education Advisory Board and Midland Recording Library for the Blind and Physically Handicapped. More recently, he served as President of the McKinney (Texas) Noon Lions Club. Walter served as a deacon and Sunday School teacher at Crestview Baptist Church in Midland, Valley Ranch Baptist Church in Valley Ranch (Texas), and at Community North Baptist Church in McKinney where he currently attends. He and his wife, Gail, reside in McKinney. They have two daughters and four grandchildren.

Both of Walter's daughters, as well as one grandson, also suffer from optic nerve atrophy, making his commitment to helping those with disabilities even more personal. In fact, his oldest daughter, Dr. Beth A. Ashby Jones, Associate Professor of Special Education at Texas A&M University–Commerce, has prepared a resource manual for parents and educators who are working with students with visual impairments which highlights the holistic needs of this population. More information can be found at walterashby.com.

CPSIA information can be obtained
at www.ICGtesting.com
Printed in the USA
LVHW011101260821
696160LV00001B/110